STUDY GUIDE

to accompany

RESEARCH METHODS
IN THE SOCIAL SCIENCES

Sixth Edition

Chava Frankfort-Nachmias
David Nachmias

PREPARED BY

KENRICK S. THOMPSON
Arkansas State University Mountain Home

WORTH PUBLISHERS

Study Guide
by Kenrick S. Thompson
to accompany
Research Methods in the Social Sciences, Sixth Edition
by Chava Frankfort-Nachmias and David Nachmias

Portions of this *Study Guide* appeared in the Second Edition, which was prepared by Robert D. Foss and Roger B. Trent, both of West Virginia University. Portions of the Third Edition were prepared by Stephen H. Wainscott of Clemson University. Portions of the Fourth Edition were prepared under the supervision of P.S. Associates, Inc.

Printed in the United States of America

ISBN: 1-57259-908-1

Printing: 4 3 2 1

Year: 03 02 01 00

Worth Publishers
41 Madison Avenue
New York, N.Y. 10010
www.worthpublishers.com

CONTENTS

PREFACE

The *Study Guide to accompany Research Methods in the Social Sciences* is intended to help students to learn to use the skills and techniques taught in the Sixth Edition of the text by Chava Frankfort-Nachmias and David Nachmias. Each chapter in this *Study Guide* is divided into a chapter abstract, objectives, main points, key terms, self-evaluation exercises, review tests, and exercises and projects.

CHAPTER ABSTRACT

The abstract gives you an overview of the basic concepts in the chapter.

CHAPTER OBJECTIVES

The objectives list the key points in each chapter. After you have reviewed a chapter in the text, you should be able to discuss each of these points in some depth, and also be able to explain their importance to and purpose in the study of social research.

MAIN POINTS

This material outlines the contents of a chapter in the text in order to do a quick review of that chapter. You should be able to expand on each of these points both in classroom discussion and in essay format for homework assignments or for classroom examinations.

KEY TERMS

The alphabetized list of important words and ideas discussed in each text chapter allows you to identify these terms and to give a definition of each. You are asked to imagine a series of "short answer" questions that ask you to define each term in your own words, using the text's discussion as a guide.

SELF-EVALUATION EXERCISES

The exercises consist of fill-in-the-blank questions, and provide a handy review of chapter contents. They should also help you to strengthen your understanding of the material. Answers are given in the answer key, but you should consult the text for a fuller explanation of any answers you are not sure you fully comprehend.

REVIEW TESTS

The reviews consist of multiple-choice and true-false questions drawn directly from the text chapters. You should answer these questions as if they made up a classroom examination, and then check your answers against those given in the answer key. Make it a point to study the material in the text for any question you may have answered incorrectly.

EXERCISES AND PROJECTS

As you master the skills and concepts in the research environment, you will want to apply what you have learned. Many of the exercises will require independent research with both primary and secondary sources. Your instructor may choose to assign the exercises as homework. Some exercises can be completed directly in this *Study Guide* by using material in the text. If you successfully complete the exercises, you will have a thorough understanding of the material in the text and will exhibit the ability to engage in research in real situations.

KST
December, 1999

CHAPTER 1

THE SCIENTIFIC APPROACH

CHAPTER ABSTRACT

In this chapter, we first define science and then compare the scientific approach with three other approaches to knowledge. We discuss the assumptions of science, its aims, and the role of methodology in the scientific approach. We define the scientific approach, first by its assumptions about nature and experience and then by its methodology relating to communication, reasoning, and intersubjectivity. We then present the ideas of scientific revolutions, discoveries, and progress. Finally, we present a model of the research process, the stages of which are discussed throughout the text.

CHAPTER OBJECTIVES

After studying this chapter, you should be able to:

1.   distinguish between science and the three alternative models of knowing: authoritarian, mystical, and purely rationalistic.

2.   define the assumptions that characterize the scientific approacn.

3.   state the aims of the social sciences.

4.   apply the rules that formulate the framework of methodology.

5.   discuss the scientific revolution, including the distinction between normal and revolutionary science.

6.   describe the research process, including each stage involved.

1

MAIN POINTS

What Is Science?

Science is frequently misunderstood and not easily defined. Science is not any general or particular body of knowledge; science is united not by its subject matter but by its methodology. Science refers to all knowledge collected by means of the scientific methodology.

Approaches to Knowledge

The scientific approach is one mode by which people have attempted to understand their environment and themselves. Three other modes are: the authoritarian mode, in which knowledge is sought by referring to those who are socially or politically defined as qualified producers of knowledge; the mystical mode, in which knowledge is obtained from such supernaturally knowledgeable authorities as prophets, gods, and mediums; and the rationalistic mode, wherein the totality of knowledge is seen as being acquired by strict adherence to the forms and rules of logic.

Basic Assumptions of Science

The philosophy of science is termed epistemology: the study of the foundations of knowledge. The assumptions associated with this philosophy are: 1) nature is orderly and regular; 2) we can know nature; 3) all natural phenomena have natural causes; 4) nothing is self-evident; 5) knowledge is derived from the acquisition of experience; and 6) knowledge is superior to ignorance.

Aims of the Social Sciences

The ultimate goal of the social sciences is to produce an accumulating body of reliable knowledge, permitting people to explain, predict, and understand empirical phenomena that are of interest. Scientific explanation provides a systematic and empirical analysis of those antecedent factors in a given situation that are responsible for the occurrence of the phenomenon. In a deductive explanation, a phenomenon is explained by demonstrating that it can be deduced from an established universal law. A probabilistic explanation makes use of generalizations that express an arithmetical ratio between phenomena or generalizations that express tendencies. Prediction is the reverse of the process of explanation; the antecedent observations merely point out that the initial conditions are present. The third component of social scientific knowledge is understanding, and the meaning of this term exists in two radically different senses.

Verstehen, or empathetic understanding, refers to a tradition in which the natural and social sciences are seen as distinctive bodies of knowledge; it involves the argument that social scientists must seek the understanding of human behavior in a subjective fashion. In contrast, logical empiricists take the position that social scientists can attain objective knowledge in the study of the natural as well as the social world (predictive understanding).

The Roles of Methodology

The scientific methodology is a system of explicit rules and procedures upon which research is based and against which claims for knowledge are evaluated. This methodology is tentative, open, self-critical, and self-correcting. Methodology involves explicit rules about communication, thus encouraging criticism and replication. The scientific methodology also demands competence in logical reasoning and analysis. The essential tool of the scientific approach, along with factual observations, is logic-- the system of valid reasoning that permits drawing reliable inferences from factual observations. Finally, methodology requires intersubjectivity, meaning that knowledge in general and the scientific methodology in particular have to be transmissible.

The Scientific Revolution

Scientific knowledge is knowledge provable by both reason and experience. Thomas Kuhn's image of the scientific enterprise includes the distinction between normal science and revolutionary science. Normal science is viewed as the routine verification of the dominant theory in any historical period. Paradigms closely relate to the idea of normal science. In contrast to normal science, Kuhn views revolutionary science as the abrupt development of a rival paradigm that can be accepted only gradually by a scientific community. Paradigm transformation is what is revolutionary in science. In sharp contrast to Kuhn's view of science is Karl Popper's prescriptive theory, wherein he maintains that the scientific community ought to be, and to a considerable degree actually is, an open society in which no dominant paradigm is ever sacred.

The Research Process

The research process consists of seven principal stages: problem, hypothesis, research design, measurement, data collection, data analysis, and generalization. The most characteristic feature of the research process is its cyclic nature. The research process is also self-correcting and represents a rational reconstruction of scientific practice.

KEY TERMS (page reference in parenthesis)
To assist you in familiarizing yourself with the Key Terms, imagine a series of "short answer" questions that ask you to define each term in your own words, using the text's discussion as a guide.

assumptions of science (5)

constructive criticism (13)

context of discovery (17)

context of justification (17)

deductive explanation (8)

empirical (6)

epistemology (5)

explanation (7)

inference (12)

interpretive approach (11)

intersubjectivity (14)

logic (13)

logical empiricists (11)

methodology (12)

normal science (15)

paradigm (15)

prediction (9)

probabilistic explanation (8)

rationalism (4)

replication (13)

research process (18)

revolutionary science (16)

science (2)

tautology (5)

Verstehen (10)

SELF-EVALUATION EXERCISES

What Is Science?

1.   Science is distinguished from other modes of inquiry by its _____
_____.

Approaches to Knowledge

2.   The word *science* is derived from Latin and means_____
_____.

3.   In the rationalistic mode of knowledge, truth is determined by_____
_____.

4.   In the mystical mode of knowledge, what is the role of logical reasoning?
_____

5.   Philosophers such as Aristotle and Immanuel Kant represent which mode of knowledge? _____

6.   True of False. Pure mathematics is an example of the authoritarian mode of knowledge.

7.   Pure geometry says nothing about reality; its propositions are _____, that is, true by virtue of their logical form alone.

Basic Assumptions of Science

8.   True or False. The assumption that nature is orderly is a fact proven by years of accumulated scientific evidence.

9.   Some fundamentalist Christians have claimed that the disease known as AIDS is a manifestation of divine punishment of homosexuality. This conflicts with the assumption of science that _____

_____.

10.   Common-sense notions of individual behavior and society conflict with the scientific assumption that _____

_____.

11.   Science is empirical; that is, scientific knowledge is based on information coming from one's _____

_____.

Aims of the Social Sciences

12.   The three aims of science are _____, _____, and _____.

13.   If a phenomenon can be explained as an instance of the working of universal law, the explanation is called _____.

14.   Probabilistic explanations differ from deductive explanations in that they

_____.

15.   The chief limitation of probabilistic explanations is that _____

_____.

16.   Empathetic or intuitive understanding of behavior is referred to as _____; an offspring of this tradition is the _____ approach.

The Roles of Methodology

17.   A system of explicit rules and procedures upon which research is based and against which claims for knowledge are evaluated is known as _____

_____.

18.   The system of reasoning that underlies all scientific methodology is called

_____.

19. A conclusion can be perfectly logical and still be erroneous if it is not related to verified _____.

20. The _____ of science refers to the fact that its reasoning and its observations can be shared with other qualified observers; they are not the personal property of the original investigator.

21. The essential tool of the scientific approach, along with factual observations, is _____ -- the system of valid reasoning that permits drawing reliable inferences from factual observations.

The Scientific Revolution

22. _____ is what Thomas Kuhn refers to as routine verification of a dominant paradigm.

23. In the conduct of normal science, _____ are discoveries which conflict with and cannot be accounted for by a dominant paradigm.

24. When anomalies to a dominant paradigm increase, a rival paradigm may be proposed. As the rival paradigm gains acceptance and the old paradigm is gradually discredited, a(n) _____ may ensue.

25. The activities of the scientist within the _____ are not constrained by methodology.

The Research Process

26. Scientific research is an enterprise which requires both _____ validity and _____ verification.

27. In what sense is scientific research cyclic?

_____

_____

_____

28. In what sense is scientific research self-correcting?

_____

_____

29. True or False. In ordinary scientific problem solving, collecting data precedes the formulation of hypotheses.

30. True or False. The research process involves seven distinct stages. To support a claim for knowledge, these stages cannot be undertaken out of sequence.

REVIEW TESTS

Multiple-Choice   Place the letter corresponding to the one BEST answer in the space provided.

_____ 1.   In a conversation with a friend, you say: "Republicans are more intelligent than Democrats. I know this because Professor Smith told me so." This statement reflects the _____ mode of knowledge.
    a.   rationalistic
    b.   authoritarian
    c.   mystical
    d.   empirical

_____ 2.   Knowledge which is derived from supernatural sources is known as the _____ mode of knowledge.
    a.   rationalistic
    b.   authoritarian
    c.   mystical
    d.   phenomenological

_____ 3.   The branch of knowledge concerned with determining the foundations of knowledge is:
    a.   metaphysics
    b.   logic
    c.   epistemology
    d.   radiology

_____ 4.   Propositions that are true by virtue of their logical form alone are termed:
    a.   tautological
    b.   metaphysical
    c.   epistemological
    d.   mystical

_____ 5.   Which of the following is NOT an assumption of science?
    a.   Knowledge is superior to ignorance.
    b.   Knowledge is derived from the acquisition of experience.
    c.   The natural world is characterized by regularity and order.
    d.   Most natural phenomena have supernatural causes.

_____ 6. Scientific knowledge is based on information coming from one's senses and observations. That is to say, it is:
    a.   self-evident and based on common sense
    b.   empirical
    c.   self-evident
    d.   superior to other modes of knowledge

_____ 7. A scientific explanation which is based upon an established universal law and which follows rules of formal logic is called a(n):
    a.   deductive explanation
    b.   probabilistic explanation
    c.   inductive explanation
    d.   normative explanation

_____ 8. Suppose it were a universal law that individuals making an income of less than $20,000 vote Democratic, while persons making $20,000 or more vote Republican. Due to heavy losses suffered by his company, John is forced to accept a pay cut from $21,000 to $19,000. Using a deductive explanation, we can say that:
    a.   it is likely that John will vote Democratic
    b.   there is a 50–50 chance that John will continue to vote Republican
    c.   John will vote Democratic
    d.   other factors must be known before any prediction can be made

_____ 9. Studies have shown that among whites, anti-black prejudice is associated with lower education. Billy Bob is a white male who dropped out of school in the eighth grade. Using a probabilistic explanation, we could say that:
    a.   Billy Bob is a racist
    b.   Billy Bob is misunderstood and has low self-esteem
    c.   it is more likely that Billy Bob is racially prejudiced
    d.   more information about Billy Bob must be known before any prediction about his racist views can be made

_____ 10.   In its explanations of human behavior, social science based on the
tradition of *Verstehen*:
  a.   is strictly empirical
  b.   applies to large human groups, but not to individual
        behavior
  c.   is essentially a biological explanation of human behavior
  d.   stresses subjective understanding

_____ 11.   Logical empiricism, as opposed to the *Verstehen* tradition, takes the
position that:
  a.   objective knowledge is possible in the study of both the
        natural and the social world
  b.   the phenomena of major concern to social scientists are more
        stable than are those of concern to natural scientists
  c.   the phenomena of major concern to social scientists are more
        replicable than are those of concern to natural scientists
  d.   the phenomena of major concern to social scientists are more
        reliable than are those of concern to natural scientists

_____ 12.   A system of explicit rules and procedures on which research is based and
against which claims for knowledge are evaluated is called:
  a.   scientific knowledge
  b.   scientific methodology
  c.   epistemology
  d.   scientific empiricism

_____ 13.   The system of valid reasoning that permits drawing reliable inferences
from factual observations is:
  a.   epistemology
  b.   methodology
  c.   logic
  d.   empiricism

_____ 14.   According to Kuhn's "scientific revolution" view, normal science is:
  a.   science within an established paradigm
  b.   the investigation of scientific anomalies
  c.   deductive problem solving without empirical data
  d.   science without an organizing principle

_____ 15.   According to Kuhn, when scientific revolutions occur:
   a.   they quickly replace dominant paradigms
   b.   they usually do so in a predictive way
   c.   the scientific community is usually discredited by the general public
   d.   they usually unfold over a long period of time

_____ 16.   To meet the test for scientific knowledge, a proposition must have:
   a.   logical validity and empirical verification
   b.   logical proof and community acceptance
   c.   common sense and ethical integrity
   d.   public value and governmental approval

_____ 17.   The activities of the scientist within the _____ are not constrained by methodology.
   a.   context of justification
   b.   empirical realm
   c.   context of discovery
   d.   qualitative realm

_____ 18.   The research process is cyclic in that:
   a.   many problems are studied more than once
   b.   findings must be continually checked through replication
   c.   social scientists must borrow from the physical sciences
   d.   it usually starts with a problem and ends with a tentative empirical generalization

True or False   Circle T if the answer is true, F if it is false.

T   F   1.   Subject matter determines whether a discipline is a science or not.

T   F   2.   Common sense is the ultimate test of scientific knowledge.

T   F   3.   Empirical knowledge is that which relies on perceptions, experience, and observation.

T   F   4.   Mathematics is an example of the rationalistic mode of knowledge.

T   F   5.   Science assumes that most natural events occur in a random fashion.

T   F   6.   The logic of prediction is fundamentally different from the logic of explanation.

T   F   7.   The *Verstehen* tradition assumes that natural science and social science use different research methods because of the different nature of their subject matter.

T   F   8.   Scientific knowledge requires only empirical verification.

T   F   9.   In the research process, stating a research hypothesis usually precedes collecting data.

T   F   10.   The research process is cyclic in that stages must be followed in exact sequence.

EXERCISES AND PROJECTS

Exercise 1–1

In either the editorial or "Letters to the Editor" section of a local newspaper, find examples of knowledge based on the authoritarian, mystical, and scientific modes of understanding. Quote the sentence or two that exemplify the mode, and then explain briefly why you classified it as you did.

<u>Authoritarian mode</u>

Example:

Explanation:

Mystical mode

Example:

Explanation:

Scientific mode

Example:

Explanation:

Exercise 1–2

Is the notion that human beings have free will consistent with the assumptions of science? Show how free will agrees with or contradicts each of the assumptions of science listed in Chapter 1.

Next, answer the question "Is social science fundamentally different from sciences that do not attempt to explain human behavior?"

Exercise 1–3

Explain how the aims of science—explanation, prediction, gaining a sense of understanding, and bettering the human condition—would be met by a scientist doing research on the following hypothesis: "Infliction of the death penalty does not reduce the homicide rate."

CHAPTER 2

CONCEPTUAL FOUNDATIONS OF RESEARCH

CHAPTER ABSTRACT

In this chapter, we will first discuss the formation of concepts, the building-blocks of theoretical systems. Then, we will distinguish four levels of theory and delineate the models that represent aspects of the real world. Finally, we will explore the links between theory and research.

CHAPTER OBJECTIVES

After studying this chapter, you should be able to:

1. be familiar with the four functions of concepts in social scientific research.

2. understand and be able to distinguish between conceptual and operational definitions, using the definitions of alienation as an example.

3. understand the significance of congruency between conceptual and operational definitions, and be able to discuss theoretical import.

4. be able to discuss the three misconceptions about theories.

5. be able to distinguish between Parson's and Shils's four levels of theory.

6. understand formal or axiomatic theory.

7. be able to describe and explain the use of models in social scientific research.

8. understand and be able to discuss the controversy of theory-then-research versus research-then-theory.

MAIN POINTS

Concepts

A concept is an abstraction representing an object, a property of an object, or a certain phenomenon. Concepts serve a number of important functions in social science research: 1) they are the foundation of communication; 2) they introduce a point of view--a way of looking at empirical phenomena; 3) they are means for classification and generalization; 4) they serve as components of theories and thus of explanations and predictions.

Definitions

Clarity and precision in the usage of concepts are achieved by definitions. Three types of definitions are important in social science research: conceptual definitions consist of primitive and derived terms. Primitive terms are those on which there is a consensus over their meaning; usually their meaning is conveyed by indicating examples. Derived terms are those that can be defined by the use of primitive terms.

Conceptual definitions are neither true nor false and they enhance communication to the extent that they: 1) delineate the unique attributes or qualities of that which is defined; 2) are not circular; 3) are stated positively; 4) use clear terms.

Operational definitions refer to sets of procedures that describe the activities one should perform in order to establish empirically the existence or degree of existence of a phenomenon described by a concept. Operational definitions are a bridge between the conceptual-theoretical and empirical-observational levels.

Concepts have both conceptual and operational components; the problem faced by the social scientist involves the integration of these two levels.

The Congruence Problem and Theoretical Import

Two important issues arise with the transition from the conceptual level to the empirical-observational level. The first is the degree of congruence between conceptual and operational definitions. The second issue involved arises when concepts cannot be operationally defined; that is, they cannot be either directly or indirectly observed. Scientific concepts should not be evaluated only in terms of their observability but also in terms of their theoretical import; that is, some concepts gain meaning only in the context of the theory in which they are introduced.

Theory: Functions and Types

Theory means different things to different people. Three common misperceptions about theory are that it is unrealistic and provides no basis for practical decision making, that it is a descriptive philosophy, and that it cannot be empirically verified.

There is no one simple definition of theory that would be agreed upon by all social scientists, and this is so because there are many different kinds of theories serving different purposes. Nachmias and Nachmias's classification is based on the Parsons and Shils distinction among four levels of theory: ad hoc classificatory systems, taxonomies, conceptual frameworks, and theoretical systems.

Ad hoc classificatory systems consist of arbitrary categories constructed in order to organize and summarize empirical observations. Taxonomies are systems of categories constructed to fit the empirical observations so that relationships among categories can be described. Taxonomies perform two important functions in social science research: 1) specification of the nature of the units and how they may be described and 2) provision of the basis for further descriptive studies. Conceptual frameworks consist of descriptive categories being systematically placed within a broad structure of explicit as well as assumed propositions. Theoretical systems combine taxonomies and conceptual frameworks, but now descriptions, explanations, and predictions are related in a systematic manner. A theoretical system consists of a set of descriptive concepts, operative concepts (variables), and a set of propositions that form a deductive system. Axiomatic theory is a type of theoretical system consisting of: 1) a set of concepts and definitions; 2) a set of existence statements that describe the situations in which the theory can be applied; 3) a set of relational statements comprising axioms and theorems; 4) a logical system for deduction.

Models

A model can be viewed as a likeness of something; it is an abstraction or representation of reality. Models delineate certain aspects of the real world as being relevant to the problem under investigation, they make explicit the significant relationships among the aspects, and they make it possible to formulate empirically testable propositions regarding the nature of these relationships. Models are tools for explanation and prediction.

Theory, Models, and Empirical Research

The social sciences rest on two major components: theory and empirical research. There is a controversy about which of these components should come first. According to one school of thought, developed by Karl Popper, theory should come first, followed by research. Robert Merton and others have argued for a research-then-theory argument, with empirical research suggesting new problems for theory, calling for new theoretical formulations, leading to the refinement of existing theories, and serving the function of verification.

KEY TERMS (page reference in parenthesis)
To assist you in familiarizing yourself with the Key Terms, imagine a series of "short answer" questions that ask you to define each term in your own words, using the text's discussion as a guide.

ad hoc classificatory system (34)   model (39)
axiomatic theory (37)   operational definition (28)
concept (24)   primitive term (27)
conceptual definition (26)   research-then-theory strategy (42)
conceptual framework (35)   taxonomy (34)
congruence (30)   theoretical import (32)
derived term (27)   theoretical system (36)
fallacy of reification (25)   theory-then-research strategy (41)

SELF-EVALUATION EXERCISES

Concepts

1.   Concepts are _____ representing objects, properties of objects, or phenomena.
2.   The general concept tree is to oak is similar as the general concept _____ is to trout.
3.   Which is the most general concept: institution of higher education, bureaucracy, social organization, Yale University? _____
4.   Saying that "society" causes poverty because "society" needs the poor is to commit the fallacy of _____.
5.   Concepts allow scientists to classify and _____ the empirical world.
6.   Concepts are the principal building blocks of _____.

Definitions

7.   Definitions that describe concepts using other concepts are called
       _____ definitions.
8.   Concepts that cannot be defined by other concepts are called
       _____ terms.
9.   The word "voting" represents a set of easily observable behaviors, which can be
       operationalized by a series of steps. As such, "voting" can be used as a(n)
       _____ term in theorizing and research.
10.   Grade point average would be a(n) _____ definition of
       student academic achievement.
11.   Concepts that cannot be operationally defined may gain meaning in the context
       of a theory; thus such concepts should also be evaluated in terms of their
       _____import.

Theory: Functions and Types

12.   Laypeople often contrast theory and _____.
13.   Theory has been confused with moral _____; in this context, the
       writings of classical scholars are erroneously identified as _____.
14.   Theories can be ranked into four types:
       1.   _____
       2.   _____
       3.   _____
       4.   _____
15.   Briefly describe the two major functions of taxonomies.
       1.   _____
       2.   _____
16.   Propositions in a conceptual framework summarize and provide
       _____ and _____ for empirical observations.
17.   List five properties of a theoretical system.
       1.   _____
       2.   _____
       3.   _____
       4.   _____
       5.   _____

18.   Give the four elements of axiomatic theory.
       1.   _____
       2.   _____
       3.   _____
       4.   _____
19.   In axiomatic theory, the criteria for the selection of axioms include consistency, _____, and the status of laws.
20.   Recent practice in axiomatic theory is to select axioms that describe direct _____ relationships.
21.   What are six advantages of axiomatic theory?
       1.   _____
       2.   _____
       3.   _____
       4.   _____
       5.   _____
       6.   _____

Models

22.   A model serves the purpose of ordering and _____ our view of reality.
23.   Models are imitations or _____ of reality.

Theory, Models, and Empirical Research

24.   Karl Popper advocated the _____-then-_____ strategy, because he believed that data alone could not serve as a logical method of theory construction.
25.   The research-then-theory strategy calls for four stages:
       1.   _____
       2.   _____
       3.   _____
       4.   _____
26.   Match each term with its definition.
       a.   fallacy of reification
       b.   ad hoc classificatory system
       c.   systematic import
       d.   ostensive definition
       e.   taxonomy
       f.   primitive terms
       g.   conceptual framework

    h.   conceptual definition
    i.   operational definition
    j.   concept
    k.   theoretical system
    l.   model

_____ (1)   An abstraction representing an object, a property of an object, or a certain phenomenon

_____ (2)   Regarding abstractions as actual phenomena

_____ (3)   Definition that describes a concept by using other concepts

_____ (4)   Cannot be conceptually defined; meaning is conveyed by examples

_____ (5)   Set of procedures that describe the activities one should perform in order to establish empirically the existence of a concept

_____ (6)   System of categories constructed to fit empirical observations so that relationships among categories can be described

_____ (7)   Systematic arrangement of descriptive categories within a broad structure of explicit and assumed propositions

_____ (8)   Abstraction that retains the essential characteristics of reality but orders and simplifies that view of reality

REVIEW TESTS

Multiple-Choice   Place the letter corresponding to the one BEST answer in the space provided.

_____ 1.   Which of the following is NOT a function of concepts?
    a.   to facilitate communication
    b.   to validate personal beliefs and opinions
    c.   to facilitate classifications and generalization
    d.   to order the empirical world

_____ 2.   Which of the following is a concept?
    a.   apple
    b.   pear
    c.   fruit
    d.   blueberry

_____ 3. If we were to define "fame" as those persons appearing on the covers of weekly news magazines, we would be using a(n):
   a.   taxonomy
   b.   ostensive definition
   c.   operational definition
   d.   conceptual framework

_____ 4. If we were to define "interest in politics" in terms of how many hours per week people spend reading newspapers and watching television news programs, and how frequently they discuss politics with friends, we would be using a(n):
   a.   conceptual definition
   b.   operational definition
   c.   primitive term
   d.   paradigm

_____ 5. Which level of theorizing would be involved if we were to ask 100 people to describe themselves as liberal, moderate, or conservative on most political issues?
   a.   ad hoc classification
   b.   taxonomy
   c.   axiomatic theory
   d.   paradigm

_____ 6. In _Democracy: The Contemporary Theories_, M. Rejai suggests five preconditions for the development of democracy: physical, religious, socioeconomic, political, and psychocultural. This scheme illustrates which level of theorizing?
   a.   ad hoc classification
   b.   taxonomy
   c.   conceptual framework
   d.   axiomatic theory

_____ 7. The most critical elements of theory are:
   a.   operational definitions
   b.   empirical measures
   c.   theorems and corollaries
   d.   concepts

_____ 8.   A theoretical system which consists of interrelated statements and
           propositions logically derived from a set of concepts and definitions is
           known as a(n):
           a.   model
           b.   paradigm
           c.   taxonomy
           d.   axiomatic theory

_____ 9.   In an axiomatic theory, propositions that are deduced from axioms and
           can be empirically tested are called:
           a.   operational definitions
           b.   variables
           c.   theorems
           d.   concepts

_____ 10. Treating concepts as though they were phenomena themselves is called:
           a.   the fallacy of reification
           b.   theorizing
           c.   operationalization
           d.   the fallacy of conceptualization

_____ 11. Which of the following statements concerning the place of theory in
           empirical research is true?
           a.   It plays a vital role in the research process.
           b.   It provides no basis for making practical decisions.
           c.   It is synonymous with moral philosophy.
           d.   It does not attempt to explain empirical phenomena.

_____ 12. Concepts serve several important functions in social science research.
           Included among these are all of the following EXCEPT:
           a.   They provide a means for transmitting perceptions and
                 information.
           b.   They offer tentative answers to research problems.
           c.   They introduce a way of looking at empirical phenomena.
           d.   They provide a means for classifying and generalizing
                 experiences and observations.

_____ 13.   In order for a complex concept such as "alienation" to be empirically researched, it must first be:

         a.   conceptually defined
         b.   stated as an axiomatic theory
         c.   modeled
         d.   given a classification system

_____ 14.   The term that describes a representation of reality that serves to order and simplify our view of reality while still representing its essential characteristics is:

         a.   theory
         b.   model
         c.   concept
         d.   axiom

_____ 15.   According to your text, which should come first—theory or empirical research?

         a.   theory, because research seldom generates new theories
         b.   theory, because research does not serve as a logical method for theory construction
         c.   research, because research helps shape the development of theory
         d.   either, because theory and research interact constantly

True–False   Circle T if the answer is true, F if it is false.

T   F   1.   Concepts are abstractions of empirical phenomena.

T   F   2.   Operational definitions provide the link between abstract concepts and empirical observations.

T   F   3.   The primary purposes of taxonomies are explanation and prediction.

T   F   4.   If a concept cannot be operationally defined, it should not be used in scientific research.

T   F   5.   Plato's philosophy of the ideal polity is an example of axiomatic theory.

T   F   6.   Conceptual definitions set forth the procedures for empirical observation of a given phenomenon.

T   F   7.   A model is an abstraction that simplifies reality while representing the essential characteristics of reality.

T   F   8.   Congruence between conceptual and operational definitions can be checked according to absolute criteria.

T   F   9.   In the formulation of axiomatic theory, one selects the largest set of axioms from which all other axioms and theorems can be derived.

T   F   10.   Most theories consist of moral philosophies and value judgments.

EXERCISES AND PROJECTS

Project 2–1

In this project you will apply your knowledge of levels of theory. First, find a journal article that reports research results. Next, tell how one or more of the levels of theory described in the text is used to help the author(s) make sense of the findings. (Hint: Most journal articles describe research in terms of more than one level of theory.)

1.   Give the full bibliographic citation of the article.
2.   Illustrate how one or more of the following are used in the article to structure the empirical findings: adhoc classificatory systems, taxonomies, conceptual frameworks, and theoretical systems.

Project 2–2

Find an empirical research report in a social science journal. Look for a research report that uses some complex concept, such as participation, modernization, or quality of life.

1.   Give the full bibliographic citation of the article.
2.   Give the concept and its conceptual definition.
3.   What are its conceptual components (dimensions), and how is each conceptually defined?
4.   What devices or techniques are used to operationalize each dimension of the concept?

CHAPTER 3

BASIC ELEMENTS OF RESEARCH

CHAPTER ABSTRACT

In this chapter, we examine how scientists formulate problems amenable to research and consider two fallacies: the ecological fallacy and the individualistic fallacy. We then define variables by type and explore the relations among them. Next we trace how hypotheses are derived. Finally, we review major guides to published research, including print sources and on-line databases.

CHAPTER OBJECTIVES

After studying this chapter, you should be able to:

1.   identify the research problems characteristic of the social sciences.

2.   define units of analysis and explain what is meant by the ecological and individualistic fallacies.

3.   distinguish among dependent, independent, control, continuous, and discrete variables.

4.   explain the various relationships between variables and describe hypotheses in terms of their magnitude and direction.

5.   construct hypotheses.

6.   identify and locate the various sources of research problems and hypotheses.

MAIN POINTS

Research Problems

All research begins with a problem, and such problems must be empirically grounded and clearly and specifically articulated.

Units of Analysis

Units of analysis are entities to which scientific concepts pertain and which influence subsequent research design, data collection, and data analysis decisions. The ecological fallacy is a kind of distortion that occurs when relationships are estimated at one level of analysis and then extrapolated to another. The individualistic or reductionist fallacy occurs when scientists draw conclusions about groups, societies, or nations based on the observation of individuals.

Variables

Research problems are conveyed with sets of concepts, which are abstractions representing empirical phenomena. In order to move from the conceptual to the empirical level, concepts are converted into variables.

The variable that the researcher wishes to explain is viewed as the dependent or criterion variable. The variable expected to explain change in the dependent variable is referred to as the independent or predictor variable.

Control variables are used to determine whether an observed association between independent and dependent variables is a spurious relationship (one that is explained by other variables). A variable is continuous if it does not have a minimal size unit. Discrete variables do have a minimal size unit.

Relations

A relation in research always means a relation between two or more variables. When two or more variables are related, changes in one variable are systematically related to changes in another. Direction refers to relations between variables being either positive or negative. A positive relation means that as values of one variable increase, values of the other also increase. A negative relation indicates that as values of one variable increase, values of the other decrease.

Relations between variables are characterized not only by direction, but also by magnitude. The magnitude of a relation is the extent to which variables covary positively or negatively. The highest magnitude of relation is a perfect relation, in which knowledge of the value of one or more independent variables determines exactly the value of the dependent variable. At the other extreme is the lowest magnitude of relation, the zero relation, where no systematic covariation between the values of an independent variable and a dependent variable can be discerned.

Hypotheses

Hypotheses are tentative answers to research problems; they are tentative answers because they can be verified only after they have been tested empirically. Research hypotheses share four common characteristics; they are clear, value-free, specific, and amenable to empirical testing.

Problems and Hypotheses and Sources of Research and Hypotheses

Problems are questions about relations among variables, and hypotheses are tentative, concrete, and testable answers. Research problems and hypotheses can be derived from theories, directly from observation, intuitively, or from a combination of these. Probably the greatest source of problems and hypotheses is the professional literature, including bibliographies, indexes, abstracts, journals, statistical sourcebooks, and research handbooks.

KEY TERMS (page reference in parenthesis)
To assist you in familiarizing yourself with the Key Terms, imagine a series of "short answer" questions that ask you to define each term in your own words, using the text's discussion as a guide.

continuous variable (52)
control variables (50)
covariation (53)
dependent variable (49)
discrete variable (52)
ecological fallacy (48)
explanatory variable (49)
hypothesis (56)
independent variable (49)

individualistic fallacy (48)
magnitude of a relation (55)
negative relation (54)
positive relation (53)
relation (53)
research problem (46)
spurious relation (50)
units of analysis (47)
variable (49)

SELF-EVALUATION EXERCISES

Research Problems

1.   The starting point of all scientific research is the _____.
2.   In the social sciences, problems must be amenable to _____.

Units of Analysis

3.   Units of analysis are _____ .
4.   Failure to make conclusions based on the appropriate unit of analysis is called the ecological fallacy--when results are obtained from studying groups but conclusions are drawn about the behavior of _____

_____ .

5.   Inappropriately drawing conclusions about groups from data on persons constitutes _____ .
6.   If we found that a large percentage of citizens of a country believe strongly in democratic values (e.g., majority rule, due process of law, individual freedoms), we could be committing the individualistic fallacy if we concluded that

_____

_____ .

7.   If we found that countries with large Communist Party membership also experienced political violence, we could be committing the ecological fallacy if we concluded that _____

_____ .

Variables

8.   What is the distinction between a concept and the variable we use to represent it?_____

_____ .

9.   If we believe that one variable is in some sense the cause of another (the effect), the presumed cause is called the _____ and the presumed effect is called the _____ .
10.   In what sense is the distinction between independent and dependent variables determined by the particular research purpose?

_____

_____ .

11.   Control variables are often used to determine whether the relationship between two variables is _____ .
12.   Distinguish between continuous and discrete variables.

_____

_____

Relations

13.   In research, a relation is a linkage between two or more _____
       _____.

14.   To say that two variables covary is to say that they _____
       _____.

15.   If high income is associated with high levels of political participation, and low
       income with low participation levels, the direction of the relation is
       _____.

16.   A negative relation means that as the value of one variable increases, the value of
       the other variable _____.

17.   The _____ of a relation is the extent to which two variables covary.

18.   In terms of magnitude, most relations encountered in social science research are
       between _____ and _____.

Hypotheses

19.   How are hypotheses distinguished from research problems?
       _____
       _____

20.   Identify the four characteristics of a workable hypothesis.
       1._____
       2._____
       3._____
       4._____

Problems and Hypotheses

21.   Which of the following propositions or questions are amenable to scientific
inquiry? (Circle your choices.)
       1.   Is extramarital sex more common among males than females?
       2.   Is extramarital sex immoral?
       3.   Will extramarital sex make one go blind?
       4.   Are people who engage in extramarital sex more likely than people who
             do not engage in extramarital sex to become divorced?
       5.   Should public school students be taught the dangers of premarital sex?
       6.   Are people who avoid extramarital sex more likely to gain eternal
             salvation than people who engage in extramarital sex?

22.   "Opinions on foreign aid are related to political party affiliation." What is wrong with this hypothesis?

_____

_____

_____.

23.   According to the text, one of the richest sources of research problems are professional _____.

24.   What do abstracts have that are not normally found in the indexes of bibliographies?

_____

_____

_____.

REVIEW TESTS

Multiple-Choice   Place the letter corresponding to the one BEST answer in the space provided.

_____   1.   The starting point of all scientific research is:
   a.   stating the problem
   b.   outlining a theory
   c.   identifying the variables
   d.   developing a research design

_____   2.   Which of the following is a variable rather than a concept?
   a.   insanity
   b.   political power
   c.   years of education
   d.   liberalism

_____   3.   Which of the following is a set of variables?
   a.   sophomore, Catholic, right-handed
   b.   female, Norwegian, blond
   c.   nonvoter, banker, divorce
   d.   income, religion, occupation

_____ 4.   If we discovered that outbreaks of political violence occur more often in democracies with large Communist Party memberships, we would be committing the ecological fallacy if we concluded that:
    a.   democracy promotes violence
    b.   communism promotes violence
    c.   communists are violent people
    d.   democracy and communism are incompatible

_____ 5.   Suppose we found that a larger percentage of Catholic than Methodist women have had abortions. We would be making an individualist fallacy if we concluded that:
    a.   the Catholic church is pro-abortion
    b.   Catholic women are sexually immoral compared to Methodist women
    c.   Catholic women are wealthier than Methodist women and therefore are better able to afford abortions
    d.   Methodist women are more conservative in their attitudes toward abortion than are Catholic women

_____ 6.   When we say that two variables covary, we mean that the:
    a.   variables are causally related
    b.   relationship between the variables is spurious
    c.   variables are unrelated to each other
    d.   variables tend to change together and have something in common with each other

_____ 7.   Consider the following hypothesis: "Degree of political participation varies with one's sense of self-esteem." In this hypothesis the independent variable is:
    a.   "degree of political participation"
    b.   "varies with"
    c.   "sense of self-esteem"
    d.   It cannot be determined from the above information.

_____ 8.   If people's income and their approval of government welfare programs are negatively related, then which of the following is true?
    a.   Poor people disapprove of welfare programs.
    b.   Wealthy people disapprove of welfare programs.
    c.   Wealthy people approve of welfare programs.
    d.   Income has no effect on approval of welfare programs.

_____ 9. A variable is dichotomous if it:
   a.   cannot be subdivided
   b.   assumes two values
   c.   assumes only one value
   d.   has a minimal-size unit

_____ 10. Which of the following is an example of a continuous variable?
   a.   the number of students in political science courses
   b.   the amount of money states spend on prison maintenance
   c.   the ages of members of Congress
   d.   the number of cars registered on college campuses

_____ 11. Suppose we observed that the greater the sales of ice cream cones, the greater the incidence of rape. We also observe that the season of the year is related to both ice cream cone sales and the number of rapes. In this case, "season" would be:
   a.   the independent variable
   b.   the dependent variable
   c.   a control variable
   d.   a dichotomous variable

_____ 12. If we discover that ice cream cone sales and the incidence of rape are both related to the season of the year, we would conclude that the original relationship between ice cream cone sales and the incidence of rape is:
   a.   spurious
   b.   causal
   c.   inverse
   d.   positive

_____ 13. Research hypotheses must be all of the following EXCEPT:
   a.   free of researchers' values
   b.   derived from previous research
   c.   testable
   d.   specific

_____ 14. Overall, which of the following is the BEST source of research hypotheses?
   a.   observation
   b.   logical deduction
   c.   professional literature
   d.   common sense

_____ 15.   "The degree of urbanization in a society varies with technological development." This statement is BEST categorized as a(n):
- a.   variable
- b.   concept
- c.   operational hypothesis
- d.   hypothesis

True-False   Circle T if the answer is true, F if it is false.

T   F   1.   Any problem that can be conceptualized can be subjected to empirical analysis.

T   F   2.   Hypotheses should be stated as generally as possible in order to enhance creativity.

T   F   3.   The ecological fallacy is committed when one makes inferences about individuals based upon data or groups.

T   F   4.   A variable is an empirical property that has three or more values.

T   F   5.   In the equation $Y = f(x)$, x is the independent variable.

T   F   6.   A spurious relation is one that shows a cause-effect relationship between two variables.

T   F   7.   The variable that the researcher wishes to explain is the independent variable.

T   F   8.   Control variables determine whether a relationship between two variables is spurious.

T   F   9.   The direction of a relation refers to whether two variables covary positively or negatively.

T   F   10. Hypotheses are statements of conclusive proof.

T   F   11. The following is a scientific hypothesis: "The national speed limit should be increased to 65 miles per hour."

T   F   12.   Most hypotheses are derived by searching the professional literature in a particular area of study.

T   F   13.   Hypotheses are expressed in the form of a relation between experimental variables and control variables.

T   F   14.   A relation in empirical research always refers to whether the relation between the variables is positive or negative.

EXERCISES AND PROJECTS

Exercise 3-1

1) Suppose a survey of adult residents in a suburban community explored the relation between personal income and attitudes toward a proposal to increase local property taxes. In the spaces provided, supply the following information:

Unit of analysis: _____
Independent variable: _____
Dependent variable: _____
Expected direction of relationship: _____
Possible control variable: _____

2) Suppose the same survey examined the relation between frequency of attendance of religious services and attitudes toward a proposed local ordinance to ban the sale of alcoholic beverages to persons under the age of 21. The relation is positive if we find that _____

_____
_____
_____ .

Exercise 3-2

For each set of three variables shown below, formulate a clear, specific, and value-free research hypothesis. Also indicate how you think the control variable could affect the relation between the independent and dependent variables.

Set A   **Independent variable:** ethnicity
         Dependent variable: trust in government
         Control variable: socioeconomic status

         Hypothesis:

         Effect of control variable:

Set B   **Independent variable:** age
         Dependent variable: voter turnout
         Control variable: interest in politics

         Hypothesis:

         Effect of control variable:

Set C   **Independent variable:** urbanization
         Dependent variable: birthrate
         Control variable: availability of birth
                                   control information

         Hypothesis:

         Effect of control variable:

<u>Set D</u>   **Independent variable:**   gender
                Dependent variable: automobile safety
                Control variable: driving distance

                Hypothesis:

                Effect of control variable:

Exercise 3-3

In terms of the criteria for hypothesis construction discussed in Chapter 3, identify the defect in each of the following statements:

1.   "Attitudes toward authority are related to childhood upbringing."

2.   "Welfare programs are the result of the moral decay of society."

3.   "Intuition is the most important key to wise decision making."

4.   "The disease AIDS is the result of divine punishment for sexual deviance."

Project 3-4

In a professional social science journal (many are listed in Chapter 3 of your text), locate an article that reports research designed to test some hypotheses.

1.   Give the full bibliographic citation for the article.

2.   What is the unit of analysis?

3.   What is the **principal** hypothesis?

4.   What is the independent variable, and how is it operationalized?

5.   What is the dependent variable, and how is it operationalized?

6.   Are the independent and dependent variables discrete or continuous?

7.   Is the relation between the independent and dependent variable positive, negative, or zero?

CHAPTER 4

ETHICS IN SOCIAL SCIENCE RESEARCH

CHAPTER ABSTRACT

This chapter discusses the ethics of conducting social science research and ways to ensure the rights and welfare of persons and communities that are the subjects of scientific studies. First, we review the reasons for recent concerns with research ethics. Next, we present three case studies--on obedience to authority, police behavior, and the attitudes of college students--as examples of some central ethical concerns. We then discuss the ethical dilemma of social scientists--the conflict between the right to research and the right of research participants to self-determination, privacy, and dignity. We also suggest a cost-benefit framework for making ethical decisions in particular situations. Informed consent and the right to privacy are important ethical issues; we discuss them next. Finally, we examine professional codes of ethics and present a composite code for social scientists.

CHAPTER OBJECTIVES

After studying this chapter, you should be able to:

1.   explain how ethical concerns become an issue in social science.

2.   discuss the costs and benefits of research that should be considered in deciding whether the benefits of a research project outweigh any potential costs.

3.   describe the nature of informed consent, including its major elements: competence, voluntarism, full information, and comprehension.

4.   discuss the dimensions of privacy.

5.   distinguish between the guarantees of anonymity and confidentiality for research participants.

MAIN POINTS

Why Research Ethics?

Ethical issues arise from the kinds of problems that social scientists investigate and the methods used to obtain valid and reliable data. As the scope of the social sciences has expanded, and as our methods of research and analysis have become more sophisticated, there has been a heightened concern with the ethics involved in social science research.

The Milgram study of obedience to authority is an important and controversial case that illustrates key ethical questions such as deception of research participants, the possibility of psychological harm being done to participants, the influence the experimentation had on participants' trust of authority figures, privacy, and the ethical implications of future research.

Balancing Costs and Benefits

The ethical dilemma of social science research involves the conflict between two rights: the right of investigators to conduct research and acquire knowledge and the right of individual research participants to self-determination, privacy, and dignity. Within the context of costs versus benefits, two central problems emerge that most often concern investigators: informed consent and privacy.

Informed Consent

There is a wide consensus among social scientists that research involving human participants should be performed with the informed consent of the participants; informed consent is absolutely essential whenever participants are exposed to substantial risks or are asked to forfeit personal rights.

The idea of informed consent derives from cultural values and from legal considerations; it rests upon the high preference we give to freedom and self-determination. Although there is now general acceptance of the principle of informed consent, there are wide variations. This is mainly a result of disagreements about what informed consent means in particular. The major elements of informed consent are competence, voluntarism, full information, and comprehension.

Privacy

The right to privacy may easily be violated during an investigation or after its completion. Privacy may be considered from three different perspectives: the sensitivity of information being given, the setting being observed, and dissemination of the information.

Anonymity and Confidentiality

Applying the right of anonymity requires that the identity of individuals be separated from the information they give.

Investigators have a strict moral and professional obligation to keep the promise of confidentiality: even though researchers are able to identify a particular participant's information, they would not reveal it publicly. Despite this obligation, there are circumstances in which it may be difficult or impossible for investigators to maintain confidentiality.

Professional Code of Ethics

The major professional societies representing social scientists have developed codes of ethics to assist their members. These codes comprise the consensus of values within the different professions and help the individual researcher to delineate and explicate what is required and what is forbidden.

KEY TERMS (page reference in parenthesis)
To assist you in familiarizing yourself with the Key Terms, imagine a series of "short answer" questions that ask you to define each term in your own words, using the text's discussion as a guide.

anonymity (78)
codes of ethics (80)
competence (73-74)
comprehension (76)
confidentiality (71)
deception (71)

ethical dilemma (72)
informed consent (72)
reasonably informed consent (75)
right to privacy (76)
sensitivity of information (77)
voluntarism (74)

SELF-EVALUATION EXERCISES

Introduction

1.   The principles and guidelines that help researchers to uphold general societal values while conducting research are called the _____ of research.

Why Research Ethics?

2.   What ethical concerns arose with the Milgram obedience experiment?
       1.   _____
       2.   _____
       3.   _____
       4.   _____
3.   Discuss the ethical issues involved in the Reiss study of police behavior.

       _____
       _____
       _____
       _____

4.   The primary ethical issue involved in the study of college student characteristics described in the text was the _____ of sensitive personal information.

Balancing Costs and Benefits

5.   Deception has become a common practice in social research, because
       _____.
6.   The two conflicting issues that frequently pose an ethical dilemma in research are:
       1.   _____
       2.   _____
7.   The two ethical problems most often of concern to researchers are _____ and _____.

Informed Consent

8.   The four elements generally agreed to be involved in obtaining informed consent are _____, _____, _____, and _____.

9.   Generally, individuals not competent to provide consent to be involved in a research project may be included anyway if a _____ provides consent and the participant is likely to _____ from the research.
10.   To be fully adequate, consent must be both _____ and

_____.

11.   It has been suggested that a researcher is most likely to obtain truly voluntary consent if he or she establishes a(n) _____ relationship with the potential participants.
12.   Because it is not always possible to provide full information to participants before they consent to be involved in research, a policy of providing _____ has been adopted.
13.   Federal government guidelines follow the principle of reasonably informed consent and call for six elements of information to be conveyed to potential research participants. What are these?
    1.   _____
    2.   _____
    3.   _____
    4.   _____
    5.   _____
    6.   _____

Privacy

14.   According to the text, the three dimensions of privacy are:
    1.   _____
    2.   _____
    3.   _____
15.   Probably the most private setting in our culture is _____.
16.   A person might be less concerned about confidentiality in a study to be published in a regional journal than in a study to be reported on national television, because in the former case, the information is _____

_____.

17.   Two methods commonly used to protect individuals' privacy are _____ and _____.

Anonymity and Confidentiality

18.   What distinguishes the assurance of anonymity from the assurance of
        confidentiality in research?

        _____

        _____

        _____.

19.   True or False. If a researcher is able to associate specific information with a
        particular individual, that individual cannot be assured of confidentiality in the
        research process.

20.   Reporting data in the form of hypothetical "average" or typical cases is called

        _____.

Professional Codes of Ethics

21.   Professional codes of ethics comprise a consensus of _____ within
        the profession.

22.   What are the five most commonly agreed upon principles of ethical research
        included in the composite code of ethics?

        1.   _____

        2.   _____

        3.   _____

        4.   _____

        5.   _____

REVIEW TESTS

Multiple-Choice   Place the letter corresponding to the one BEST answer in the space
                      provided.

_____ 1.   In the conduct of social science research, ethical considerations are LEAST
               likely to be evoked by the:

               a.   setting in which the research takes place
               b.   method of data collection
               c.   amount of time it takes to collect data
               d.   kinds of individuals serving as research participants

_____ 2. The major ethical issue of the Milgram study was that:
   a. subjects were asked to provide information of a sensitive and personal nature
   b. the experimental participants were subjected to physical harm
   c. the researcher failed to provide research participants with a guarantee of confidentiality
   d. the participants were initially deceived as to the true purpose of the study

_____ 3. The Reiss study of police brutality has been criticized on ethical grounds because:
   a. the researchers encouraged police officers to brutalize citizens
   b. the police officers were misled about the nature of the study
   c. the researchers unwittingly incited citizens to riot
   d. the identities of several officers were divulged to their superiors

_____ 4. The American Council of Education study of college students received criticism on the grounds that:
   a. the anonymity of the participants was not safeguarded
   b. the purpose of the study was not clearly defined
   c. the sample was restricted to student activities
   d. the survey participants were subjected to emotional stress

_____ 5. Informed consent is absolutely essential in research in which:
   a. participants are exposed to risk or are forfeiting personal rights
   b. experimental research designs are used
   c. participants are subjected to physical stimuli
   d. personal interviews are used

_____ 6. In social science research, what is considered to be ethical is based primarily on:
   a. state and federal law
   b. sets of moral absolutes
   c. the subjective judgment of the researcher
   d. court guidelines

_____ 7.   Which of the following is the most accurate statement about how
            decisions relating to the ethics of research should be made?
            a.   Researchers should follow the advice of a lawyer.
            b.   An individual judgment should be made on the basis of the
                  costs and benefits in each case.
            c.   Laws are clearly spelled out and researchers should follow
                  them.
            d.   If there is any potential for harm to a participant, the
                  research should not be conducted.

_____ 8.   The idea of informed consent derives from:
            a.   the assumption that the value of knowledge outweighs
                  possible risks to research participants
            b.   Western values of obedience to authority
            c.   the high value placed on freedom and self-determination
            d.   the mystique that Americans attribute to scientific inquiry

_____ 9.   To study the effects of academic achievement on career orientation, a
            professor arbitrarily gives failing grades to a sample of students. This
            would raise the ethical concern of the:
            a.   selection of the research topic
            b.   method of data collection
            c.   kinds of individuals studied
            d.   procedures required by the research design

_____ 10.   A professor explains in detail the nature of a research project and then
            offers extra credit to students who agree to act as research subjects.
            Ethically, which issue of informed consent does this situation raise?
            a.   competence
            b.   voluntarism
            c.   full information
            d.   privacy

_____ 11.   Which of the following types of information would be LEAST likely to
            require safeguards to protect the privacy of research participants?
            a.   religious preference
            b.   income
            c.   age
            d.   sexual practices

_____ 12.   The strategy of providing reasonably informed consent involves all of the following EXCEPT:
    a.   a description of the benefits to be expected
    b.   answers to questions about research procedures
    c.   a careful explanation of the expected findings of the study
    d.   an explanation that the participant is free to withdraw from the study at any time without penalty

_____ 13.   The Humphreys study of homosexual encounters in public restrooms involved ethics because:
    a.   the privacy of those studied was not safeguarded
    b.   homosexual behavior is an inappropriate topic for social science research
    c.   the physical location of the research was inappropriate
    d.   the participants were deceived about the purpose of the study

_____ 14.   The major ethical problem with the study reported in Vidich and Bensman's _Small Town in Mass Society_ was that:
    a.   several townspeople were injured in the experiment
    b.   the townspeople's privacy was not adequately protected
    c.   the researchers misused sensitive information
    d.   informed consent was not obtained

_____ 15.   The major professional societies of social scientists have generally:
    a.   left ethical decisions to the discretion of individual researchers
    b.   avoided ethical decisions because they are too controversial
    c.   developed codes of ethics to assist their members
    d.   adopted stringent codes of ethics with severe penalties for violators

True-False   Circle T if the answer is true, F if it is false.

T   F   1.   Questions of ethics in social science research can easily be resolved by reference to moral absolutes.

T   F   2.   In an anonymous survey, the researcher is unable to identify a given response with a given respondent.

T   F   3.   The Milgram study has been regarded as unethical mainly because it subjected participants to electrical shock.

T   F   4.   Research that employs deception has become commonplace because it offers methodological and practical advantages.

T   F   5.   Ethical considerations are evoked only during the data-collection stage of research.

T   F   6.   The meaning of informed consent is clearly spelled out in laws and court decisions on the issue.

T   F   7.   The sensitivity of information refers to how personal or how potentially threatening that information is.

T   F   8.   A respondent in a personal interview must always be assured of anonymity.

T   F   9.   Access to data can be provided to people other than the original researchers without compromising a promise of confidentiality.

T   F   10.   Assuring research participants of confidentiality is the same as guaranteeing anonymity.

EXERCISES AND PROJECTS

Exercise 4-1

In order to study altruism, a researcher interviews 500 individuals about their charitable behaviors. To check the accuracy of certain responses, he persuades officials of local charities to provide the names of those who have donated during the past year. Results indicate that over 40 percent of those who say they have donated to these charities have not actually done so. The researcher writes an article discussing the implications of this fact for solicitation of donations, and the article is published in a professional journal. He also releases the results of his study to the local newspapers and provides names of the "liars" to the directors of the local charities so that they can contact these people and ask for the donations they claim to have made.

1.   What, if any, ethical issues are involved here?

2. How might the researcher have handled this project in a more ethically acceptable fashion?

3. Would you say the study should have been done at all? Why or why not?

Exercise 4-2

A researcher wishes to conduct a study of the effects of a person's upbringing on the likelihood of that person's becoming a child abuser. She plans to interview people and talk about their parents' child-rearing practices. She will also try to interview a third person (an old family friend or relative, for example) who can independently report on how a person's parents raised him or her and on whether that person is abusive to his or her children. Finally, the researcher will collect information from official records and interview family physicians in an attempt to obtain valid, reliable data on the actual incidence of child abuse.

1. List the potential costs of this project to the individuals involved.

2. List the potential benefits of this project to the participants as well as to society in general.

3. In view of the costs and benefits you listed, would you consider this research project acceptable on ethical grounds and important enough to be conducted? Why or why not?

4. If you answered no to Question 3, suggest a way to redesign the project to make it more acceptable without rendering it a useless project.

CHAPTER 5

RESEARCH DESIGNS: EXPERIMENTS

CHAPTER ABSTRACT

In this chapter, we discuss the research design as a logical model of causal inference and distinguish among several research designs. In the first section, we give an example of how an experimental research design is implemented. In the second section, we explain the structure of experimental designs. We then examine the four components of research designs: comparison, manipulation, control, and generalizability. Finally, we present some commonly used experimental designs.

CHAPTER OBJECTIVES

After studying this chapter, you should be able to:

1.   describe the research design and the classic experimental design.

2.   discuss causal inferences, including the distinct operations of demonstrating covariation, eliminating spurious relations, and establishing the time order of the occurrences.

3.   describe the four components of a classic research design: comparison, manipulation, control, and generalizability.

4.   distinguish between external and internal validity.

5.   describe the types of threats to the internal validity of experiments and the different methods of controlling these threats.

6.   define and give examples of the three major types of research designs.

MAIN POINTS

The Research Design: An Example

Once the research objectives have been determined, the hypotheses explicated, and the variables defined, the researcher confronts the problem of constructing a research design through which the hypotheses can be tested. A research design is a logical model of causal inference; it is a plan for collecting, analyzing, and interpreting data.

The Classic Experimental Design

The classic research design consists of two comparable groups: an experimental group and a control group. Randomization ensures the comparability of these groups. Both groups are pretested on the dependent variable; then the experimental group is exposed to the independent variable. Finally, a posttest of the dependent variable is conducted so that the groups can be compared. If the experimental group displays pretest-posttest differences that are unlike those of the control group, then strong evidence exists that the independent variable affects the dependent variable.

Causal Inferences

In practice, the demonstration of causality involves three distinct operations: demonstrating covariation, which means that the variables involved are associated or correlated; eliminating spurious relations, meaning that the relationship cannot be explained by some third factor; and establishing the time order of the occurrences, meaning that the independent variable actually occurred before the dependent variable.

Components of a Research Design

The classic research design consists of three components: comparison, manipulation, and control. To the extent that other factors can be ruled out as rival explanations of the observed association between the variables under investigation, the results have internal validity.

Extrinsic factors that threaten internal validity are selection factors: initial differences between experimental and control groups that may account for the differences observed in the dependent variable. Intrinsic factors that threaten internal validity include changes in the individuals or the units studied that occur during the study period, changes in the measuring instrument, and the reactive effect of the observation itself. Major threats to internal validity are history, maturation, experimental mortality, instrumentation, testing, regression artifact, and interactions with selection. Extrinsic and intrinsic factors that threaten the internal validity of causal inferences may be controlled by three procedures: matching, randomization, and the use of control groups.

The external validity of research designs consists of the generalizability of research findings. The two main issues of external validity are the representativeness of the sample and reactive arrangements in the research procedure.

Design Types

Three major types of research designs can be distinguished: experimental, quasi-experimental, and correlational/preexperimental.

The classic experimental design allows for pretest, posttest, and control-group/experimental-group comparisons; it permits the manipulation of the independent variable and thus the determination of the time sequence; and, most significantly, by including randomized groups, it controls for most sources of internal validity. However, this design is generally weak on external validity and does not allow for generalizations to be made to nontested populations. There are two variations of this design that are stronger in this respect.

The Solomon four-group design yields results that are more generalizable than the classic experimental design. It involves the same features as the classic design plus an additional set of control and experimental groups that are not pretested, thus ruling out sensitization effects.

The posttest-only control group design is a variation of both the classic design and the Solomon design; it omits the pretested groups altogether.

Factorial designs are more complicated than the classic experimental design and its variations, but they enable the researcher to study the simultaneous effects of two or more independent variables. The main advantage of factorial designs is that the generalizability of research findings is greatly increased. Another advantage is that this design allows for the systematic assessment of how two or more independent variables interact.

KEY TERMS (page reference in parenthesis)
To assist you in familiarizing yourself with the Key Terms, imagine a series of "short answer" questions that ask you to define each term in your own words, using the text's discussion as a guide.

classic research design (90)
comparison (94)
control (95)
control group (90)
covariation (93)
experimental group (90)
experimental mortality (96)
external validity (101)
extrinsic factors (95)
factorial design (108)
history (96)

instrumentation (97)
internal validity (95)
manipulation (95)
matching (99)
maturation (96)
posttest (90)
pretest (90)
randomization (100)
regression artifact (97)
research design (88-89)

SELF-EVALUATION EXERCISES

Introduction

1. A research design is a blueprint for research that guides the investigator in the process of _____, _____, and _____ observations.

The Research Design: An Example

2. In the *Pygmalion in the Classroom* study, how did the investigators make sure that "potential bloomers" and "normal students" were comparable at the beginning of the experiment?

    _____
    _____
    _____

The Classic Experimental Design

3. In the classic experimental design, the two comparable groups are called the _____ group and the _____ group.

4. In the electronic information sharing study, the communication mode in the experimental group was the _____.

5. Even though two variables covary (that is, are related to each other), why can we not automatically assume that they are causally related?

    _____

    _____

    _____

Causal Inferences

6. Besides covariation, we must demonstrate (1) that the relation cannot be explained by some other factor (is not __spurious__) and (2) that the independent variable actually occurred __before__ (before/after) the dependent variable.

Components of a Research Design

7. Describe what is meant by each of the following aspects of the classic experimental design, and tell why each is necessary.

    1. Comparison _____

        _____

        _____

    2. Manipulation _____

        _____

        _____

    3. Control _____

        _____

        _____

8. If rates of lung cancer are higher (or lower, for that matter) among smokers than among nonsmokers, we can conclude that smoking and lung cancer are

    _____.

9. Manipulation of the independent variable is difficult to accomplish in natural settings, but it is easily done in a(n) _____ setting.

10. Extrinsic factors that threaten internal validity are related to the _____ of cases (subjects) for the research.

11. Events occurring between the pretest and posttest sometimes provide explanations to rival the hypothesis. This threat to internal validity is known as

    _____.

12. The maturation threat to internal validity involves _____ or _____ changes that occur in subjects during the course of the study.

13. When study units drop out selectively from the experimental or control group during a study, a threat to internal validity known as _____ occurs.

14. Instrumentation threats to internal validity derive from _____ in the measuring instrument.

15. If study units are changed by the pretest procedures, _____ poses a threat to internal validity.

16. When study units have been selected for participation in an experiment on the basis of their extreme scores on the dependent variable, a threat to internal validity stemming from _____ occurs.

17. When selection is combined with another threat to internal validity, such as history or maturation, a new class of threats to internal validity called _____ occurs.

18. Two methods of controlling factors that threaten the internal validity of causal explanations are _____ and _____.

19. The method of matching in which a person in the experimental group is matched with an identical person in the control group is called _____.

20. Precision matching often results in the loss of a large number of cases, because _____.

21. Ensuring that the experimental and control groups have equal proportions of males and females, blacks and whites, and adults and children is an example of _____ matching.

22. The problem that arises because people cannot be matched on factors a researcher is unaware of can be solved by using the _____ method of controlling for variables.

23. Randomization involves using some method (such as tossing a coin) of ensuring that cases have a(n) _____ chance of being assigned to either the experimental or the control group.

24. Randomization and matching are methods to control for the effects of _____ factors, whereas a control group serves to control for the effects of _____ factors in a research design.

25. A study of the political party preferences of voters between the ages of 19 and 24 would lack _____ if we tried to generalize to the voting-age population.

Design Types

26.   Three major types of research design are _____, _____, and _____.

27.   Usually, quasi-experimental designs lack opportunities for _____ or _____.

28.   The two variations of the classic experimental design that are stronger in external validity are called the _____ design and the _____ design.

29.   The Solomon four-group design involves four groups rather than the two that are used in the classic experimental design. How do the two additional groups differ from the basic control and experimental groups?

_____

_____

_____

30.   The Solomon-four group design is an improvement on the classic experiment in that it allows one to assess the extent to which there is _____ due to pretesting.

31.   How does the posttest-only control-group design differ from the Solomon four-group design?

_____

_____

_____

32.   The posttest-only control-group design controls for all of the _____ sources of invalidity.

33.   A research design that includes all possible combinations of values of more than one independent variable is called a(n) _____ design.

34.   A factorial design allows us to assess how two (or more) independent variables _____.

35.   Explain what is meant by the term "interaction effect."

_____

_____

_____

36.   Factorial designs are frequently more useful than other designs because they allow a researcher to examine the _____ effects of more than one independent variable.

REVIEW TESTS

Multiple-Choice   Place the letter corresponding to the one BEST answer in the space provided.

_____ 1.   Which of the following is NOT a function of research designs?
   a.   guiding the process of collecting, analyzing, and interpreting data
   b.   enabling the researcher to draw inferences of cause-effect relationships
   c.   selecting a topic for research
   d.   determining whether research findings can be generalized to a large population or to different situations

_____ 2.   Which of the following is NOT essential for proving the existence of causal relationship between two variables?
   a.   showing that the variables are associated
   b.   establishing that the independent variable occurs prior to the dependent variable
   c.   showing that the association is not the result of some other factor
   d.   demonstrating that the findings obtained can be generalized to larger populations and different settings

_____ 3.   In an experimental research design, manipulation allows us to determine:
   a.   whether research participants have been deceived as to the nature of an experiment
   b.   the time order of the independent and dependent variables
   c.   whether two variables are associated
   d.   whether an observed association is spurious

_____ 4.   If we were to observe that people on high-cholesterol diets have higher blood pressure than people on low-cholesterol diets, we could conclude that:
   a.   cholesterol intake and blood pressure are associated
   b.   high cholesterol causes high blood pressure
   c.   the relationship between cholesterol intake and blood pressure is spurious
   d.   high blood pressure causes high cholesterol

_____ 5.   In an experimental research design, the purpose of setting up
            experimental and control groups is to demonstrate:
            a.   comparison
            b.   manipulation
            c.   control
            d.   generalization

_C_ 6.   Internal validity is a question of:
            a.   comparison
            b.   covariation
            c.   control
            d.   manipulation

_A_ 7.   In experiments, external validity involves the issue of whether:
            a.   findings obtained in one setting can be generalized to other
                  settings
            b.   a given independent variable is the cause of a given
                  dependent variable
            c.   the time sequence of the independent and dependent
                  variables has been established
            d.   concepts are being accurately measured by the independent
                  and dependent variables

_____ 8.   Generally, experimental research designs are weakest in:
            a.   comparison
            b.   manipulation
            c.   control
            d.   generalization

_____ 9.   To study the impact of a new federal law enforcement program on
            reducing drug trafficking, you select a sample of major U.S. cities that led
            the nation in drug arrests in 1984, before the program was implemented.
            In 1986, after the crackdown began, you find that drug arrests in these
            cities dropped. If you conclude that the new law enforcement program
            caused the decline in drug arrests, you could be criticized for ignoring the
            effects of:
            a.   history
            b.   subject mortality
            c.   sensitivity to testing
            d.   regression artifacts

_____ 10.   Which of the following is generally the MOST desirable method for the control of extrinsic factors?
       a.   randomization
       b.   frequency distribution matching
       c.   precision matching
       d.   generalizing

_____ 11.   The use of matching to control extrinsic factors is difficult when:
       a.   subjects volunteer to be included in the experimental group
       b.   the number of relevant factors to be controlled is large
       c.   the Solomon four-group research design is used
       d.   the posttest-only control group research design is used

_____ 12.   Suppose you are conducting an experiment on the effects of reading romance novels on attitudes toward marriage. Prior to receiving the posttest, John's fiancé breaks their engagement. If John decides to continue with the experiment, which of the following could threaten the internal validity of your experiment?
       a.   history
       b.   maturation
       c.   experimental mortality
       d.   regression artifacts

_____ 13.   In the experiment described in Question 12, what threat to internal validity might be presented if John and other jilted lovers decided to discontinue their participation in the experiment?
       a.   history
       b.   testing
       c.   experimental mortality
       d.   instrumentation

_____ 14.   What is the major difference between the classic experimental design and the Solomon four-group design?
       a.   No posttest is administered in the Solomon four-group design.
       b.   The Solomon four-group employs no control groups.
       c.   The Solomon four-group adds an experimental group and a control group, neither of which is pretested.
       d.   The Solomon four-group uses four experimental groups, each of which receives a different posttest.

_____ 15.   Which of the following research designs allows the researcher to assess the effects of more than one independent variable?
    a.   the classic experiment
    b.   the factorial design
    c.   the posttest-only control group design
    d.   the double-blind experiment

True-False   Circle T if the answer is true, F if it is false.

T   F   1.   If, in an experiment, the control and experimental groups show the same amount of change between the pretest and the posttest, one can generally assume that the independent variable had no effect on the dependent variable.

T   F   2.   Intrinsic factors are those threats to internal validity that occur prior to the research operation.

T   F   3.   If a research design is internally valid, we can be assured that it is externally valid.

T   F   4.   In conducting a classic experiment, it is important that members of the experimental and control groups be as much alike as possible.

T   F   5.   In research design, comparison is used to demonstrate the time order of the independent and dependent variables.

T   F   6.   Permitting individuals to volunteer for participation in an experiment could jeopardize internal validity through extrinsic factors.

T   F   7.   History refers to all that has happened to people prior to the time they become experimental subjects.

T   F   8.   Experimental mortality occurs when subjects drop out of experiments.

T   F   9.   Precision matching is more efficient than frequency distribution matching.

T   F   10.   Randomization controls for the effects of factors that the researcher may not even be aware of.

T   F   11.   The purpose of the Solomon four-group is to determine how much change in experimental subjects between a pretest and a posttest is due to reactive effects.

T   F   12.   The advantage of the posttest-only control group design is that it eliminates reactivity to testing.

T   F   13.   The main disadvantage of factorial designs is that they are weak in terms of generalizability.

T   F   14.   Factorial designs permit examination of the effects of more than one independent variable.

T   F   15.   Generalization primarily addresses the problem of intrinsic factors in the research operation.

EXERCISES AND PROJECTS

Exercise 5-1

A company is planning an antismoking campaign for its employees who indicated on their job application that they smoke. The management has decided that all smoking employees will participate in a series of seminars conducted by local health officials. As a consultant for this project, you suggest that the campaign would be more effective if, in addition to attending the seminars, employees are sent a personal letter from the president of the company encouraging them to stop or cut down on their smoking.

1.   What is your research hypothesis?

2.   What is the independent variable?

3.   What is the dependent variable?

4.   Which is the experimental group?

5.   Which is the control group?

Exercise 5-2

You are conducting a classic experiment on the effects of pornography on male perceptions of women. You have two groups of subjects, experimental and control, of 50 men each. Both groups will take a pretest measuring of their perceptions of women. Then, over the period of a week, the experimental group will be shown six hours of X-rated films depicting explicit sexual activity. About a week after the experimental subjects have seen the films, both groups will be posttested and compared with respect to their changed perceptions of women. Suggest and explain possible situations which could cause the internal validity of your research to be threatened by each of the following factors:

1. Selection

2. History

3. Maturation

4. Experimental mortality

5. Regression artifact

6. Test reactivity

Explain in detail how this experiment could be modified using a Solomon four-group.

Project 5-3

For this project, you are to conduct a field experiment using a factorial design. The topic to be studied is helping behavior. The particular dependent variable we will use here is giving change for a quarter. In each condition of the experiment, you are to ask a stranger for change for a quarter and then record whether he or she makes some effort to help (such as checking their pockets or asking someone else to help you). The independent variables to be examined are (1) recipient "social status" and (2) sex of helper. You can set up two conditions of social status as follows: For a "high-status" condition, dress neatly and conservatively when asking for help; for a "low-status" condition, dress sloppily. Sex of helper is manipulated by asking either males or females for change, depending on which condition of your design you are collecting data for. The design will look like this:

Recipient Social Status
High   Low

Sex of Helper
Male   Female

Within each of the four conditions, you should ask for help from 10 people. Be sure to work out a method for getting people into the experimental conditions randomly (you may want to ask you instructor for some help on this). Use the following space to report on your experiment.

1.   How did you assign people to the experimental condition?

2.   Describe briefly how you manipulated the independent variable of recipient social status.

3.   How might the dependent variable have been measured using more than the two categories "helped" and "didn't help"?

4.   What percentage of males helped? _____
      What percentage of females helped? _____
      Did sex of the people who were asked for help influence helping behavior? _____

5.   What percentage of "high-status" people were helped? _____
      What percentage of "low-status" people were helped? _____
      Did the social status of the person needing help influence helping behavior? _____

6.   Fill out the following table, giving the percentage of people who helped in each of the experimental conditions.

Recipient Social Status
High   Low

Sex of Helper
Male   Female

7.   Was there an interaction between the independent variables in this experiment? If so, describe what it was.

8.   Write a brief report presenting the conclusions of your study. Briefly discuss why this study might be lacking in internal and external validity.

CHAPTER 6

RESEARCH DESIGNS:

CROSS-SECTIONAL DESIGNS

AND QUASI-EXPERIMENTAL DESIGNS

CHAPTER ABSTRACT

In this chapter, we present a number of designs that are more common in the social sciences. First, we look at the relationship between the types of variables we study and the research designs we employ. We then discuss cross-sectional designs, quasi-experimental designs, and preexperimental designs. We also discuss combined designs, and we end by comparing the strengths and weaknesses of the various designs.

CHAPTER OBJECTIVES

After studying this chapter, you should be able to:

1. describe the kinds of relationships that lend themselves to study with cross-sectional and quasi-experimental designs.

2. discuss the respective strengths and weaknesses of cross-sectional versus quasi-experimental designs.

3. differentiate among the major types of quasi-experimental designs (contrasted groups, planned variation, time-series, control-series, and combined) and compare and contrast these techniques in terms of their strengths and weaknesses.

4. explain preexperimental designs, including the one-shot case study.

MAIN POINTS

Introduction

The controlled experiment allows the most unequivocal evaluation of causal relationships between two or more variables. However, many phenomena that are of interest to social scientists are not amenable to the straightforward application of experimental designs. Quasi-experiments, cross-sectional designs, and pre-experiments are designs that are generally weaker on internal validity and have limited causal inferential powers.

Types of Relations and Designs

Stimulus-response relationships are well suited for experimental investigation, but property-disposition relationships are not. There are four reasons for this; in stimulus-response situations: 1) the interval between cause and effect is generally short; 2) the independent variable is often specific and easy to identify; 3) it is quite simple to create groups that differ according to exposure to the independent variable but that are similar otherwise; and 4) it is easy to determine whether the independent variable actually occurred first.

Cross-Sectional Designs

The cross-sectional design is perhaps the most predominant design employed in the social sciences. This design is often identified with survey research. The most common alternatives to experimental methods of control and the drawing of causal inference in cross-sectional designs are multivariate analytic techniques such as cross tabulation and path analysis. In cross-sectional designs, researchers cannot establish time-order of the variables by performing statistical analyses; but rather, this must be done on the basis of theoretical and logical considerations.

Quasi-Experimental Designs

Quasi-experimental designs are weaker on internal validity than experimental designs, and like cross-sectional designs, they depend on data analysis techniques as a method of control and do not require randomization. They are superior to cross-sectional designs because they usually involve the study of more than one sample, often over an extended period of time.

In contrasted-groups designs, researchers observe a dependent variable in various groups that differ on independent variables. This design is weak on internal validity, but often researchers succeed in compensating for this fault by the use of matching, by expanding the number and variety of contrasted groups, or by making repeated observations of the dependent variable.

Planned variation designs are similar to contrasted groups designs, except that in the former, a stimulus, such as a program, is systematically presented to varying groups with different characteristics. Planned variation techniques are most effective when important variables are equally distributed across the groups involved.

Time-series designs involve a number of observations of the dependent variable both before and after the introduction of the independent variable. This type of design generally allows researchers to rule out testing and maturation as possible explanations for changes after the introduction of the independent variable. History and regression effects are harder to rule out, particularly if the researcher has not made many observations over a long period of time.

In control-series designs, time series are developed both for the "experimental" group and for a number of "control" groups that appear to be essentially equivalent to the "experimental" group. The groups are not really equivalent, because they were not formed by randomization. Still, they provide some protection against the threats to internal validity of history, maturation, and testing.

Combined Designs

All quasi-experimental designs have certain weaknesses. At times, researchers can effectively combine two or more of these designs in the same investigation in order to allow the strengths of one to compensate for the weaknesses of another. This may entail the development of smaller-scale experiments within a large quasi-experimental framework.

Preexperimental Designs

Preexperimental designs are not suitable for experimental manipulations and do not allow for the random allocation of cases to an experimental and a control group. In fact, most often these designs do not include a comparison group. Preexperiments are the weakest kinds of research designs since most of the sources of internal and external validity are not controlled for. The risk of drawing causal inferences from preexperimental designs is extremely high, and they are primarily useful as a basis for pretesting some research hypotheses and for exploratory research.

An example of a preexperimental design is the one-shot case study, which involves an observation of a single group or event at a single point in time, usually subsequent to some phenomenon that allegedly produced change. This technique is useful in exploratory research and may lead to insights that, in turn, could be studied as research hypotheses.

A Comparison of Designs

Two extremely basic problems in scientific research are inferring causation and generalizing the findings, and these problems pose an equally basic dilemma: in order to secure unambiguous evidence about causation, researchers frequently sacrifice generalizability. This is the problematic relationship between internal and external validity. Designs that are strong on internal validity tend to be weak on external validity, and vice versa.

Experimental designs and their counterparts tend to be internally valid but hard to generalize from, whereas surveys and some of the "weaker" quasi-experimental designs tend to be less internally valid but easy to generalize from. The contrast hinges largely on whether randomization or representative sampling is used and on the artificiality of the research setting. The dilemma of internal versus external validity can be partly resolved by using representative samples of well-defined populations in experiments and by seeking additional information to rule out certain rival hypotheses in survey investigations.

KEY TERMS (page reference in parenthesis)
To assist you in familiarizing yourself with the Key Terms, imagine a series of "short answer" questions that ask you to define each term in your own words, using the text's discussion as a guide.

combined designs (129)
contrasted groups (119)
control-series design (128)
cross-sectional design (116)
extended time-series design (125)
one-shot case study (131)

panel (123)
planned variation (122)
property-disposition relationship (115)
stimulus-response relationship (115)
time-series design (124)

SELF-EVALUATION EXERCISES

Introduction

1.   Experiments are often not feasible because of _____, _____, and _____ considerations.

Types of Relations and Designs

2.   Experiments are appropriate for studying a relationship between a(n) _____ and a(n) _____, whereas some quasi-experimental designs are used to examine a relationship between a _____ and a(n) _____.

3.   Describe how stimulus-response relationships differ from property-disposition relationships in terms of the following factors:

   1.   Time interval:

   _____

   _____

   _____

   2.   Degree of specificity:

   _____

   _____

   _____

   3.   Nature of comparison groups:

   _____

   _____

   4.   Time sequence of events:

   _____

   _____

   _____

Cross-Sectional Designs

4.   Cross-sectional designs are sometimes referred to as _____ studies.

5.   How do cross-sectional designs compensate for their lack of experimental control?

_____

_____

_____

6.   Cross-sectional studies, such as a study of the role of political orientations in determining attitudes toward economic reform in Mexico, are frequently used to study the relationships between _____ and _____.

7.   Two alternatives to experimental methods of control and the drawing of causal inference in cross-sectional designs are _____ and

_____.

8.   The main advantages of cross-sectional designs are:
       1.   _____
       2.   _____

Quasi-Experimental Designs

9.   Quasi-experimental designs are like cross-sectional designs in that they do not require _____.

10.   Quasi-experiments have greater internal validity than _____, but less than _____.

11.   In contrasted-groups designs, differences on an independent variable are examined among a large number of different _____.

12.   Four ways to strengthen the internal validity of contrasted-groups designs are to:
       1.   _____
       2.   _____
       3.   _____
       4.   _____

13.   The _____ is a more elaborate design for contrasted groups in which two or more intact groups are compared before and after the introduction of the treatment variable.

14.   The planned variation design works best when major variables are distributed _____ among the various groups involved.

15.   The panel most closely resembles which quasi-experimental design?

_____

16.   What are the main problems of panel studies?
       1.   _____
       2.   _____
       3.   _____

17.   In the time-series design, one obtains at least _____ sets of measurements before and after the introduction of the _____ variable.

18.   How can a time-series design enable you to separate reactive effects from the effects of an independent variable?

_____

_____

_____

19.   How can regression effects lead to incorrect causal inferences from a time-series design?

_____

_____

_____

20.   Control-series designs are simply time-series designs with the addition of:

_____

_____.

Combined Designs

21.   Combined designs are those that mix elements of _____ designs with elements of _____ designs.

Preexperimental Designs

22.   What are four weaknesses of preexperimental designs?
       1.   _____
       2.   _____
       3.   _____
       4.   _____
23.   Preexperiments are useful primarily for _____ research.
24.   What does the pretest-posttest design have that the one-shot case study lacks?

_____

25.   The findings of several single-case studies can be integrated by use of the:

_____.

A Comparison of Designs

26.   According to an old saying, survey researchers aren't sure what they know but do know to whom it applies, whereas experimentalists are sure of what they

know but don't know to whom it applies. What does this mean in terms of major types of designs and in terms of internal and external validity?

_____

_____

_____

_____

REVIEW TESTS

Multiple-Choice   Place the letter corresponding to the one BEST answer in the space provided.

_____ 1.   The kind of relationship that lends itself best to experimentation is:
  a.   stimulus-response
  b.   property-disposition
  c.   pretest-posttest
  d.   independent-dependent

_____ 2.   The relationship between socioeconomic status and attitudes toward social welfare programs is an example of a(n):
  a.   stimulus-response relationship
  b.   experimental research design
  c.   property-disposition relationship
  d.   pretest-posttest

_____ 3.   Quasi-experimental designs are more likely to be used when:
  a.   the causal order of the independent and dependent variables is clearly defined
  b.   relationships of the stimulus-response variety are to be explored
  c.   comparison groups are easy to establish
  d.   the interval between the independent and dependent variables is extended over a long period of time

_____ 4. Cross-sectional designs attempt to emulate experimental methods of control primarily through:
   a. random assignment of subjects to experimental methods and control groups
   b. manipulation of the independent variable
   c. multivariate methods of statistical analysis
   d. demonstrating the causal order of the independent and dependent variables

_____ 5. The most common type of research design encountered in social science is the:
   a. one-shot case study
   b. cross-sectional design
   c. planned variation design
   d. two-control-group experiment

_____ 6. In the contrasted-groups design, differences observed among groups may be due to any of the following EXCEPT:
   a. testing
   b. regression
   c. equivalence
   d. maturation

_____ 7. Planned variation designs entail:
   a. several observations both before and after the appearance of the independent variable
   b. applying the independent variable at various levels to a number of different groups
   c. equivalent experimental and control groups
   d. systematic variations in the independent variable

_____ 8. A particular strength of the panel design is that it:
   a. rules out testing effects
   b. is actually an experiment
   c. reduces the problem of getting respondents to cooperate, because so little is required of them
   d. helps establish the time order of variables

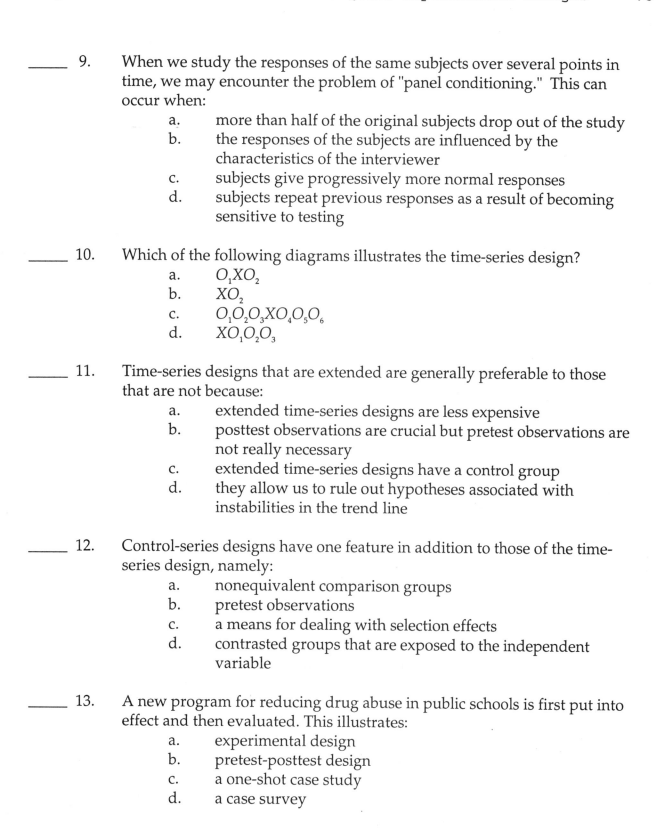

_____ 9.   When we study the responses of the same subjects over several points in time, we may encounter the problem of "panel conditioning." This can occur when:
     a.   more than half of the original subjects drop out of the study
     b.   the responses of the subjects are influenced by the characteristics of the interviewer
     c.   subjects give progressively more normal responses
     d.   subjects repeat previous responses as a result of becoming sensitive to testing

_____ 10.   Which of the following diagrams illustrates the time-series design?
     a. $O_1 X O_2$
     b. $X O_2$
     c. $O_1 O_2 O_3 X O_4 O_5 O_6$
     d. $X O_1 O_2 O_3$

_____ 11.   Time-series designs that are extended are generally preferable to those that are not because:
     a.   extended time-series designs are less expensive
     b.   posttest observations are crucial but pretest observations are not really necessary
     c.   extended time-series designs have a control group
     d.   they allow us to rule out hypotheses associated with instabilities in the trend line

_____ 12.   Control-series designs have one feature in addition to those of the time-series design, namely:
     a.   nonequivalent comparison groups
     b.   pretest observations
     c.   a means for dealing with selection effects
     d.   contrasted groups that are exposed to the independent variable

_____ 13.   A new program for reducing drug abuse in public schools is first put into effect and then evaluated. This illustrates:
     a.   experimental design
     b.   pretest-posttest design
     c.   a one-shot case study
     d.   a case survey

_____ 14.   Which of the following research designs is the WEAKEST in terms of permitting causal inferences?
   a.   the panel study
   b.   the one-shot case study
   c.   the contrasted-groups design
   d.   the planned variation design

_____ 15.   Removal from real-life situations and difficulty in generalizing to a specific population are major criticisms of:
   a.   experiments
   b.   preexperiments
   c.   quasi-experiments
   d.   correlational designs

True-False   Circle T if the answer is true, F if it is false.

T   F   1.   In examining property-disposition relations, it is fairly easy to randomly assign units of analysis to experimental and control groups.

T   F   2.   Correlational designs are most often identified with experiments.

T   F   3.   In correlational designs, control is achieved by manipulation of the stimulus or independent variable.

T   F   4.   An advantage of quasi-experimental designs is that they usually involve the study of more than one sample.

T   F   5.   The contrasted-groups design compares the dependent variable in a number of different groups or categories.

T   F   6.   Applied to survey research, the panel study's main objective is to examine change in different groups of respondents over a period of time.

T   F   7.   In time-series designs, the more measurements of the dependent variable you get, the stronger your design.

T   F   8.   The one-shot case study is more useful for generating hypotheses than for testing them.

T   F   9.   As a general rule, designs strong on internal validity tend to be weak on external validity, whereas designs weak on internal validity tend to be strong on external validity.

T   F   10.   It is generally considered more important for a design to have internal validity than external validity.

EXERCISES AND PROJECTS

Exercise 6-1

The Voting Rights Act of 1965 is generally considered to have been instrumental in ending most forms of racial discrimination in voting, especially in the southern states. Illustrate how you would employ a time-series design to study the impact of the Voting Rights Act on rates of black voter registration in the South. In designing your study, address the following questions:

1.   What is your unit of analysis?

2.   What is your dependent variable?

3.   At what time intervals would you measure the dependent variable?

4.   What potential threats to interval validity would you anticipate?

5.   How could your study be improved by employing a control-series design? For what reasons might you decide to use a control-series design?

Project 6-2

In a reputable social science journal, locate an article that uses a cross-sectional design and provide the following information:

1.   Bibliographic information (article title, journal, date)

2.   What are the independent and dependent variables?

3.   Is the relationship under study of the stimulus-response or property-disposition variety? Explain your answer.

4. In your view, does the author adequately rule out factors other than the independent variable as the "cause" of the dependent variable? Why or why not?

5. What are the article's major findings?

6. Could this research have been conducted using an experimental design? If so, how? If not, why not?

Exercise 6-3

Consider a hypothetical study designed to address a practical problem in medical care for indigent people—indigents who are hypochondriacs. Hypochondriacs are particularly a problem where people receive cheap or free medical care and where there is little incentive not to make frequent appointments to see a doctor, even though the complaints are minor.

Say we have a sizable pool of people who receive free health care at a large metropolitan hospital. Someone comes up with a way to help relieve the system of part of the load created by multiple visits of hypochondriacs: furnish them a hotline where they can get medical advice quickly, easily, and on a 24-hour-per-day basis. The hotline will be operated by interns who have been specially trained and selected to be sympathetic listeners. (This is necessary because we suspect that many hypochondriacs really are looking for someone to listen to their problems).

For the test period, we will open the hotline only to 50 patients who have been identified by doctors as extreme examples of "hypochondria." The subjects are thus selected on the criterion that they are the worst cases available. These 50 are given the hotline number and information on how it works. At the end of a 12-month test, researchers go back to patient records to look for a change in the number of visits made to the doctor. It turns out that the 50 made a mean of 1.6 visits during the 12-month test. During the 12 months before the hotline was opened, this same group visited an average of 4.3 times. On the basis of this difference, the researchers conclude that the hotline did indeed reduce the number of visits.

Consider how the researchers may have made a logical error in attributing the drop to the hotline program. How might the results be explained by (1) history, (2) maturation,

(3) testing, (4) instrumentation, (5) statistical regression, (6) selection biases, and (7) experimental mortality?

    1.   History:

    2.   Maturation:

    3.   Testing:

    4.   Instrumentation:

    5.   Statistical regression:

    6.   Selection biases:

    7.   Experimental mortality:

CHAPTER 7

MEASUREMENT

CHAPTER ABSTRACT

In this chapter, we explore the nature of measurement in the social sciences and discuss the concept of isomorphism, which concerns how measurement instruments relate to the reality being measured. We then present the four levels of measurement: nominal, ordinal, interval, and ratio. Next, we discuss the issue of measurement error. The chapter concludes with descriptions of the concepts of validity--whether an instrument measures what it is supposed measure--and reliability--whether, and by how much, measurements are consistent from one observation to the next.

CHAPTER OBJECTIVES

After studying this chapter, you should be able to:

1.   define measurement and explain its nature and structure.

2.   list the four levels of measurement and the differences among these levels, and tell why these distinctions are important.

3.   define validity, name the three basic kinds of validity, and distinguish among these types.

4.   define reliability and describe the methods of assessing it.

MAIN POINTS

The Nature of Measurement

Measurement is closely related to the concept of operational definitions. Measurement is a procedure in which one assigns numerals--numbers or other symbols--to empirical properties (variables) according to a set of rules. Numerals are symbols, Roman or Arabic, that are given quantitative meaning and then become numbers that make possible the use of mathematical and statistical techniques for purposes of description, explanation, and prediction. Assignment refers to the mapping of symbols onto objects or events. Rules explicate the ways in which numerals or numbers are to be assigned to objects or events.

Rules are the most significant component of the measurement procedure because they determine the quality of measurement. Poor rules make measurement meaningless. Isomorphism means similarity or identity of structure. In measurement, the crucial question to be asked is whether the numerical system is isomorphic with the structure of the concepts being measured. Frequently, social scientists measure indicators of concepts, and often multiple indicators must be developed to represent abstract concepts.

Levels of Measurement

The requirement of isomorphism between numerical systems and empirical properties (or indicators) leads to a distinction among different ways of measuring--that is, to distinct levels of measurement.

The lowest level of measurement is the nominal level, where numbers or other symbols are used to classify objects or observations. A nominal level of measurement is attained when a set of objects can be classified into categories that are exhaustive and mutually exclusive.

Measurements at the ordinal level involve exhaustive and mutually exclusive categories, but the categories are also rank ordered from high to low. The assignment of symbols is arbitrary, but ordinal measurements are rank ordered.

The interval level of measurement involves difference, ranking, and equal intervals between categories; thus, the unit measurement is constant across the scale.

At the ratio level of measurement, the ratio of any two numbers is independent of the unit of measurement; this measure has all of the components of the interval level but involves natural zero points.

Data Transformation

Variables that can be measured at a ratio level can also be measured at the interval, ordinal, and nominal levels. As a rule, properties that can be measured at a higher level can also be measured at lower levels, but not vice versa.

Measurement Error

Differences in scores that are due to anything other than real differences in the aspects of the property being measured are termed measurement errors. Measurement errors result when the scores obtained are related to an associated attribute, or they may be due to differences in temporary conditions, in the setting, or in the administration of the measuring instrument. They may also result when different people interpret the instrument in different ways.

Systematic measurement errors are constant between cases and studies, whereas random errors affect the results differently each time the measuring instrument is used.

Validity

Validity is concerned with the question: "Is one measuring what one thinks one is measuring?" There are different types of validity.

Content validity means that the measurement instrument covers all the attributes of the concept or phenomenon you are trying to measure. There are two common varieties of content validity: face validity and sampling validity. Face validity rests on the investigators' subjective evaluation as to the validity of a measuring instrument. Sampling validity is concerned with whether the content of the instrument adequately represents the content population of the property being measured. Empirical validity is concerned with the relations between a measuring instrument and the measurement of outcomes; if a measuring instrument is valid, then there should exist strong relations between the results produced by the instrument and other variables. Predictive validity is estimated by a prediction to an external measurement, referred to as a criterion, and by checking a measuring instrument against some outcome.

Construct validity involves relating a measuring instrument to a general theoretical framework in order to determine whether the instrument is tied to the concepts and theoretical assumptions that are employed.

Reliability

Reliability is a central concern to social scientists because it is rare when measuring instruments are completely valid. A frequently used method for evaluating an instrument is its degree of reliability. Reliability refers to the extent to which a measuring instrument contains variable errors. Each measure consists of two components: a true component and an error component. Reliability is defined as the ratio of the true-score variance to the total variance in the scores as measured.

There are three common methods for estimating measurement reliability: the test-retest method, the parallel-forms technique, and the split-half method.

KEY TERMS (page reference in parenthesis)
To assist you in familiarizing yourself with the Key Terms, imagine a series of "short answer" questions that ask you to define each term in your own words, using the text's discussion as a guide.

construct validity (152)
content validity (149)
empirical validity (150)
face validity (150)
generalizability (157)
indicator (142)
interval level (146)
isomorphism (141)
known-groups technique (153)
measurement (138)
measurement errors (149)

nominal level (143)
ordinal level (144)
parallel-forms technique (156)
predictive validity (151)
ratio level (147)
reliability (154)
reliability measure (155)
sampling validity (150)
split-half method (156)
test-retest method (155)
validity (149)

SELF-EVALUATION EXERCISES

The Nature of Measurement

1. In the measurement process, what does the researcher assign to empirical properties according to rules?
   1. _____
   2. _____
   3. _____
2. In measurement, when numerals are given quantitative meaning, they are called _____ *numbers* _____ .
3. Assignment is the process of _____ symbols onto objects or events.
4. Measurement rules specify _____ .

5. When the structure of a measurement seems very similar to the reality it purports to represent, that measurement is said to be _____ with reality.

6. Measurement in the social sciences is often less _____ than in the physical sciences; that is, social scientists more often measure the _____ rather than the properties themselves.

7. To the extent that indirect indicators must be used, the researcher has to make large _____ leaps to reach conclusions.

Levels of Measurement

8. The four levels of measurement are _nominal_, _ordinal_, _interval_, and _ratio_.

9. The level of measurement in which numerals are used solely for purposes of classification is called _nominal_.

10. The minimum requirements for nominal measurement are that all categories must be _exhaustive_ and _mutually exclusive_

11. When the categories of a variable not only are exhaustive and mutually exclusive but also permit rank ordering, the researcher has achieved a(n) _ordinal_ level of measurement.

12. In addition to exhibiting the properties of nominal and ordinal scales, interval scales have categories that are _interval_.

13. The ratio level of measurement is characterized by a true _zero_ as well as all the properties of the other levels of measurement.

Data Transformation

14. Differences in measurement scores can be attributed to _____ in the aspects of the property being measured or to measurement errors.

15 List five sources of measurement errors.

1. _____

2. _____

3. _____

4. _____

5. _____

16. Measurement errors that are constant between cases and studies are termed _____ errors. Those that affect usage of the measurement instrument in a different way are called _____ errors.

Validity

17.   Validity involves the question of whether _____

_____.

18.   The three basic kinds of validity are _____, _____, and

_____.

19.   _____ validity involves the researcher's subjective judgment that an instrument measures what it is intended to measure.

20.   The primary concern of sampling validity is whether _____

_____.

21.   The correlation between a measurement instrument and a specified outcome of the measure indicates the _____ validity of the measure.

22.   The type of validity that involves the relationship of a measuring instrument to an overall theoretical framework is _____.

Reliability

23.   Every measurement consists of two components: a(n) _____ and a(n) _____. The ratio of these two components indicates the _____ of a measure.

24.   When the reliability coefficient is zero, one can conclude that the measure is _____.

25.   The three common methods of estimating the reliability of a measuring instrument are the _____ method, the _____ method, and the _____ method.

26.   Explain the two limitations of the test-retest method of reliability assessment.

1.   _____

2.   _____

27.   The _____ technique is a means of overcoming the limitations of the test-retest method of estimating reliability.

28.   The _____ method of assessing reliability involves separating a measuring instrument into two parts and examining the correlation between these parts.

REVIEW TESTS

Multiple-Choice   Place the letter corresponding to the one BEST answer in the space provided.

_D_ 1. The process of measurement involves the assignment to observations of any of the following EXCEPT:
    a.   numerals
    b.   numbers
    c.   symbols
    d.   concepts

_B_ 2. To say that a measure is isomorphic is to say that:
    a.   the numbers assigned to observations imply actual quantities
    b.   the numerical system of the measurement has a structure similar to the structure of the concept being measured
    c.   it can be transformed to any level of measurement
    d.   it is part of a set of multiple indicators of a concept

_A_ 3. Measurements in which numerals are used to classify objects are called:
    a.   nominal
    b.   ordinal
    c.   interval
    d.   ratio

_C_ 4. Ordinal measurement allows us to:
    a.   classify objects only
    b.   rank objects only
    c.   classify and rank objects only
    d.   classify and rank objects and also specify by how much one object is greater than another object

interval

_D_ 5. Suppose we assigned persons a number from 1 to 7 as a measure of their patriotism, with 7 representing the "most patriotic." Which of the following statements can we assume to be true?
    a.   A person assigned a 6 is twice as patriotic as a person assigned a 3.
    b.   The difference between a person with a 7 and a person with a 5 is the same as the difference between a person with a 3 and a person with a 1.
    c.   Persons assigned 5, 6, or 7 are more likely to vote than persons assigned 1, 2, 3, or 4.
    d.   A person assigned a 6 is more patriotic than a person assigned a 5.

__A__ 6.   If we used the following numerals to measure religious preference—1-Catholic, 2-Jewish, 3-Muslim, 4-Protestant—a person assigned a 4 is:
   a.   likely to be a Protestant
   b.   likely to be more religious than an individual assigned a 3
   c.   more likely than a person assigned a 2 to disagree with the teachings of Catholicism
   d.   likely to be a Catholic

__C__ 7.   The altitude (in feet) of cities from sea level is an example of a(n) _____ measurement.
   a.   nominal
   b.   ordinal
   c.   interval
   d.   ratio

__D__ 8.   The amount of time in minutes it takes for students to complete this review test is an example of a(n) _____ measurement.
   a.   nominal
   b.   ordinal
   c.   interval
   d.   ratio   *zero*

__B__ 9.   A room thermometer that also measures relative <u>humidity</u> accurately and consistently is, with respect to its intended purpose as a measure of temperature:
   a.   valid but not reliable
   b.   reliable but not valid
   c.   valid and reliable
   d.   neither valid nor reliable

(It measures two different variables)

__A__ 10.   Two thermometers, A and B, each show a temperature 300• F. When the wind velocity is 10 miles per hour, thermometer A reads 280• while thermometer B remains at 300•. We can conclude that:
   a.   thermometer A is valid but unreliable
   b.   thermometer B is valid but unreliable
   c.   thermometer A is unreliable while B is invalid
   d.   thermometer A is invalid while B is unreliable.

validity but not reliable

_B_ 11. A researcher develops a set of items to measure student satisfaction with college. The measure is then shown to several university guidance counselors to determine if the items measure the concept the researcher intends to measure. The researcher is seeking to establish the _____ of the measure.
- a. reliability
- b. face validity
- c. precision
- d. predictive validity

_C_ 12. A researcher develops a measure of "religiosity" in which survey respondents are asked questions about the importance of religion and the value of prayer and confession in their daily lives. Which of these BEST tests the predictive validity of the original measure?
- a. asking the respondents to indicate their denominational preference (Catholic, Protestant, Jewish, etc.)
- b. asking whether the respondents approve of organized prayer in public school
- c. asking respondents how often they attend religious services
- d. asking respondents whether they are Republicans or Democrats

_A_ 13. Which of the following methods of estimating reliability corresponds MOST CLOSELY to the conceptual definition of reliability?
- a. the test-retest technique
- b. the multitrait-multimethod technique
- c. the parallel-forms technique
- d. the split-half technique

 14. If we were assessing the validity of a scale designed to measure predisposition to become a child abuser, which type of validity would we be MOST concerned with?
- a. content validity
- b. empirical validity *predictive*
- c. construct validity
- d. sampling validity

devise

_D_ 15. Each of the following is a common source of error in measurement procedures EXCEPT:

     a.   the scores obtained are related to an associated attribute.

     b.   Different people interpret the measurement in different ways. ✓

     c.   Temporary conditions, such as health or mood, affect a person's responses or behavior. ✓

     d.   The data derived from the procedures are not statistically significant. ✓ → *results*

True-False   Circle T if the answer is true, F if it is false.

T   F   1.   To measure something, one must assign to observations numbers that are amenable to mathematical manipulation.

T   F   2.   Rules for assigning numerals or numbers to objects are the most important aspect of measurement.

T   F   3.   To be isomorphic the structure of a measure must be similar to the structure of arithmetic.

T   F   4.   Statistical operations that can be performed to one level of measurement are permissible for all other levels of measurement.

(T)   F   5.   A variable which was originally measured at the ordinal level can be converted into a nominal variable. (1st) (2nd) OK

T   (F)   6.   Numbers used to represent ordinal measurement indicate absolute quantities.

(T)   F   7.   Ratio measures have an arbitrary zero point.

(T)   F   8.   To assess the face validity of a measure, one must rely completely on subjective judgments.

T   (F)   9.   Predictive validity is the most widely used test of the construct validity of a measure. *criterion*

(T)   F   10.   Construct validity involves determining how a measure fits within a broad theoretical framework of interrelated concepts.

(T)   F   11.   It is possible for a measure to be reliable but not valid.

(T)   F   12.   If a survey researcher suspects that respondents are simply
                   remembering and repeating the same responses they gave in a
                   previous survey that used the same questions, the test-retest
                   method will overestimate the reliability of a measure.

OK (T)   F̸   13.   The split-half method of determining reliability requires two forms
                   of a measurement instrument that are parallel.
                   ↳ equal measurement

(T)   F   14.   According to Cronbach et al., the chief concern of reliability theory
                   is generalizability—how universal the sets of measurement are.

T   F̸   15.   Reliability refers to the relations between a measuring instrument
                   and the measurement outcomes.

EXERCISES AND PROJECTS

Exercise 7-1

After each description of a process given below, indicate the level of measurement
(nominal, ordinal, interval, or ratio) implied by the statement.

1.   Asking people which television network they watch the most often: ABC,
      CBS, NBC, Fox, or CNN. _____

2.   Asking people how much time during the week they spend watching
      television news programs: more than 10 hours, 7 to 10 hours, 3 to 6 hours.
      _____

3.   Rating members of Congress as very liberal, slightly liberal, moderate,
      slightly conservative, or very conservative. _____

4.   Asking members of Congress how much campaign money they have
      received from political action committees (PACs). _____

5.   Asking members of Congress whether the amount of money they have
      received from PACs is more than $100,000, between $50,000 and $100,000,
      or less than $50,000. _____

6.   Asking members of Congress the source of most of their PAC
      contributions: labor unions, corporate management, medical associations,
      or civil rights groups. _____

7. Asking members of Congress which of the following they feel is the most important problem facing the country today: the budget deficit, the threat of nuclear war, crime, poverty, or teen pregnancy. _____

8. Asking members of Congress if they think the amount of money the government is spending on AIDS research should be increased, kept the same, or decreased. _____

9. Checking the *Congressional Record* to see how many times in the past year members of Congress were absent from roll-call votes. _____

10. Asking members of Congress to indicate whether they are Democrats or Republicans. _____

Exercise 7-2

You are in charge of a study of the attitudes of adult males toward affirmative action programs for women. One-half of the sampled males are interviewed by female interviewers, the other half by male interviewers. The results of your survey show that males interviewed by female interviewers have a higher approval of affirmative action programs than the subjects interviewed by male interviewers. Assuming that all subjects answered the same questions, what can you most likely conclude about your measure of affirmative action attitudes?

Exercise 7-3

You are involved in a study of antiblack prejudice and discrimination in state political party organizations. You decide to measure your key variable, racial prejudice and discrimination, by (a) attending party organization meetings and observing whether conversations between blacks and whites seem to be friendly or hostile, and whether whites seem to pay attention to speeches made by blacks; and then (b) examining state party directories and calculating the percentage of leadership positions held by blacks. Which measurement method is more reliable? Which is more valid? Explain your answer below.

Exercise 7-4

In considering levels of measurement, we often think that variables can be measured at only one level. However, it is frequently possible to measure a given variable at two or more levels. For example, although we usually think of age as a ratio variable, we could transform age into an ordinal variable by placing individuals into several age groupings, such as 18, 19–25, 26–40, and so on. Your task is to indicate whether (and if so, how) each of the following variables might be measured at different levels. In some instances, you may have to use your imagination!

1.   Smoking

Nominal:
Ordinal:
Ratio:

2.   Gender

Nominal:
Ordinal:
Ratio:

3.   Socioeconomic status

Nominal:
Ordinal:
Ratio:

4.   Intelligence

Nominal:
Ordinal:
Ratio:

5.   Political modernization

Nominal:
Ordinal:
Ratio:

CHAPTER 8

SAMPLING AND SAMPLE DESIGNS

CHAPTER ABSTRACT

In this chapter, we cover the fundamentals of sampling theory, the how and why of sample selection. In the first section, we discuss the aims of sampling. We then move on to definitions and a discussion of central concepts--population, the sampling unit, sampling frame, and the sample--as well as the procedures of probability and nonprobability designs. Next, we discuss the considerations involved in determining the sample size. Finally, we present procedures for estimating nonsampling errors.

CHAPTER OBJECTIVES

After studying this chapter, you should be able to:

1.   discuss the aims of sampling, including how samples are utilized in describing populations.

2.   describe the various types of sample designs, distinguish between probability and nonprobability sampling procedures, and explain the pros and cons of each procedure.

3.   describe the major types of probability sampling, their strengths and weaknesses, and how to select a sample using each method.

4.   explain the dynamics of sample size, including standard error and confidence interval.

5.   cite the factors that introduce nonsampling errors into an investigation.

MAIN POINTS

Aims of Sampling

Sampling is a technique utilized by researchers to make inferences about a large body of data (population) on the basis of a smaller body of sample data. A particular value of the population is called a parameter; its counterpart in the sample is termed a statistic. The major objective of sampling theory is to provide accurate estimates of unknown parameters from sample statistics that can be easily calculated. In order to estimate accurately unknown parameters from known statistics, three major problems must be dealt with effectively: 1) the definition of the population, 2) the sample design, 3) the size of the sample.

Population

A population is the "aggregate of all cases that conform to some designated set of specifications." A sampling unit is a member of a population the traits of which we wish to investigate. A sample may be drawn from an infinite or from a finite population. Sampling designed to produce information about particular characteristics of a finite population is called survey sampling and is typical of social research.

Once the population has been defined, a sample that adequately represents the population may be drawn. The actual procedures involve selecting a sample from a complete list of sampling units. The list of the sampling units used to select the sample is called a sampling frame. Typical problems in sampling frames include 1.) incomplete frames (some units are missing), 2.) clusters of elements (groups of units are listed rather than individual units), and 3.) blank foreign elements (some units on the list should not be in the population).

Sample Designs

The essential requirement of any sample is that it be as representative as possible of the population from which it is drawn.

In modern sampling theory, a basic distinction is made between probability and nonprobability sampling. The distinguishing characteristic of probability sampling is that one can specify for each sampling unit of the population the probability that it will be included in the sample. In nonprobability sampling, there is no way of specifying the probability that each unit has of being included in the sample, and there is no assurance that every unit has some chance of being included.

Social scientists do employ nonprobability samples, even though accurate estimates of the population's parameters can be had only through probability samples. Nonprobability samples are utilized when convenience and economy are demanded, when a sampling population cannot be precisely defined, and when a list of the sampling population is unavailable. Three major designs of nonprobability samples have been used by social scientists: convenience samples (researcher selects whatever sampling units are conveniently available); purposive samples (researcher selects sampling units that, in his or her judgment, are representative of the population); and quota samples (selection of a sample that is as similar as possible to the sampling population). Snowball samples.

Probability sample designs include simple random sampling, systematic sampling, stratified sampling, and cluster sampling. Simple random sampling is the basic probability sampling design and is incorporated into all the more elaborate probability designs. This technique involves numbering all population elements and then selecting sufficient random numbers to compile a sample of desired size; it is simple but is inconvenient to implement with large populations.

Systematic sampling consists of selecting every Kth sampling unit of the population after the first sampling unit is selected at random from the first K sampling units. Systematic sampling is more convenient than simple random sampling, especially when a population is very large or when large samples are to be selected.

Stratified sampling is used primarily to ensure that different groups of a population are adequately represented in the sample, so that the level of accuracy in estimating parameters is increased; it reduces the cost of execution considerably. Sampling from the different strata can be either proportional (the number of elements selected from each stratum is proportional to that stratum's representation in the population) or disproportional (sometimes chosen in order to yield sufficient numbers in a stratum to allow intensive analysis of that particular stratum).

Cluster sampling is frequently used in large-scale studies because it is the least expensive sample design; it involves first the selection of larger groupings, called clusters, and then the selection of the sampling units from the clusters. The clusters are selected by a simple random sample or a stratified sample. The choice of clusters depends upon the research objectives and the resources available for the study.

Sample Size

A sample is any subset of sampling units from a population. A subset is any combination of sampling units that does not include the entire set of sampling units that has been defined as the population. The idea of standard error is central to sampling theory and to the understanding of how to determine the size of a sample. When an infinite number of independently selected sample values (such as means) are placed in a distribution, the resulting distribution is called the sampling distribution of the mean, and its standard deviation is the standard error. The mean of all the sample values in a sampling distribution is an unbiased estimate of the population value, and the standard error allows the researcher to determine the probability that a given sample estimate is close to the actual population value.

Assuming that a distribution of sample statistics is approximately normal, researchers can use the standard deviation of the normal curve to place a confidence interval around their sample statistic.

Nonsampling Errors

Sampling theory is concerned with the error introduced by the sampling procedure. In a perfect design, this error is minimized for an individual sample. The error in estimates refers to what is expected in the long run if a particular set of procedures is followed. However, even if the sampling error is minimized, there are other sources of error. In survey research, the most pervasive error is the nonresponse error: those observations that are not carried out because of refusal to answer, not-at-homes, lost forms, and so on. Nonresponse can introduce a substantial bias into the findings.

KEY TERMS (page reference in parenthesis)
To assist you in familiarizing yourself with the Key Terms, imagine a series of "short answer" questions that ask you to define each term in your own words, using the text's discussion as a guide.

cluster sample (173)
confidence interval (179)
nonprobability sample (167)
nonresponse error (182)
parameter (163)
population (163)
probability sample (167)
representative sample (167)
sample (163)

sampling frame (165)
sampling unit (164)
simple random sample (169)
standard error (177)
statistic (163)
stratified sample (172)
subset (177)
systematic sample (171

SELF-EVALUATION EXERCISES

Introduction

1.   Samples are used in order to make accurate _____ about a larger
_____ .

Aims of Sampling

2.   In survey research in particular, sampling is usually necessary because
_____
_____
_____ .

3.   A particular value of a population is known as a(n) _____ , while its
counterpart value in a sample is called a(n) _____ .

Population

4.   An aggregate of a defined population is called a(n) _____ .
5.   A sample member of a defined population is called a(n) _____ .
6.   Survey populations with a countable number of sampling units are termed
_____ populations.
7.   Telephone directories and employee rosters are examples of _____ .
8.   Researchers generally try to find a supplemental list when they are faced with
a(n) _____ sampling frame.
9.   When sampling units are listed in _____ rather than individually, it
is often possible to sample these and then to sample individual sampling units
within them.
10.   When a sampling frame contains _____ , it is best to compensate by
drawing a larger sample.
11.   Explain the reasons for the *Literary Digest*'s inaccurate prediction of the 1936
presidential election. _____
_____
_____
_____

Sample Designs

12.   The main requirement of any sample is that it be _____
        _____
        _____.

13.   What distinguishes probability sampling from nonprobability sampling?
        _____
        _____
        _____
        _____

14.   What are some of the circumstances that would call for the use of nonprobability
        sampling?
        _____
        _____
        _____
        _____

15.   If you interviewed the first 50 students who entered the library after 8:00 p.m.,
        you would be using a _____ sample.

16.   The old saying about presidential elections, "As Maine goes, so goes the nation,"
        reflects the basic concept of the _____ sample.

17.   What are three shortcomings of quota sampling?
        1.   _____
        2.   _____
        3.   _____

18.   The major types of probability sampling are _____, _____,
        _____, and _____.

19.   In a simple random sample of 50 drawn from a population of 300, the probability
        of selection for each element is n/N, or _____.

20.   The advantage of systematic sampling over simple random sampling is that it is
        _____
        _____.

21.   In what way may systematic samples be susceptible to bias?
        _____
        _____

22.   If one wishes to make sure that specific groups of a population are adequately
        represented in a sample, _____ sampling should be used.

23.   If we drew a sample of 50 males and 50 females from a population known to be
        60 percent male and 40 percent female, we would be employing
        _____ stratified sampling.

24.   What are some of the advantages of cluster sampling?

_____

_____

_____

Sample Size

25.   The size of a sample should be estimated by taking into consideration

_____

_____.

26.   The amount of variation between a sample statistic and a population parameter
       is the _____.

27.   The standard error is estimated by dividing the _____ by the

_____.

28.   A finite population correction factor must be included in the calculation of the
       standard error when _____

_____.

29.   The confidence we can have that a sample mean falls within a certain range is the
       _____.

30.   What proportion of all sample means will fall (1) within plus or minus 1 standard
       error of the sampling distribution? _____ (2) within plus or minus 2
       standard errors? _____

31.   When a confidence interval is narrow, the probability that the population mean
       is not actually contained by the interval is _____ (small/large).

Nonsampling Errors

32.   In survey research, the most pervasive error is due to _____.

33.   In what way was the inaccuracy of the *Literary Digest*'s 1936 presidential election
       prediction due to nonresponse bias?

_____

_____

_____

_____

34.   The four types of nonresponse, each affecting sample results differently, are
       _____, _____, _____, and _____.

REVIEW TESTS

Multiple-Choice   Place the letter corresponding to the one BEST answer in the space provided.

_____ 1.   The number of registered voters in Dade County, Florida, as of January 1, 1987 would be considered a(n):
    a.   finite population
    b.   infinite population
    c.   sampling unit
    d.   parameter

_____ 2.   In a study of homicide rates in 400 counties randomly selected from all U.S. counties, the sampling unit consists of:
    a.   perpetrators of homicides
    b.   weapons
    c.   homicide victims
    d.   counties

_____ 3.   Using a telephone directory as a sampling frame can lead to a problem because many people choose to keep their names and phone numbers unlisted. This problem is known as:
    a.   blank foreign elements
    b.   clusters of elements
    c.   an incomplete frame
    d.   a nonprobability sample

_____ 4.   The key feature of probability sampling is that:
    a.   smaller samples are required
    b.   larger samples are required
    c.   sampling error is eliminated
    d.   each sampling unit's probability of selection is known

_____ 5.   If it is impossible to estimate the representativeness of a sample, it is a:
    a.   probability sampling design
    b.   disproportionate stratified sample
    c.   nonprobability sampling design
    d.   systematic random sample

_____ 6.   If each member of a population is represented by a uniquely numbered Ping-Pong ball, and a portion of the balls are blindly drawn from a large bin after being well mixed, the result is a:
    a.   simple random sample
    b.   quota sample
    c.   convenience sample
    d.   cluster sample

_____ 7.   You are conducting research entitled "Attitudes of Black Americans Toward the Economic Policies of the Bush Administration." To carry out your research you administer questionnaires to members of the local chapter of the NAACP. This would be an example of a:
    a.   cluster sample
    b.   stratified sample
    c.   quota sample
    d.   purposive sample

_____ 8.   You wish to take a sample of students at your college or university that is highly representative of the student population in terms of gender, class, rank, and major. Which sampling design would be the BEST to use in this situation?
    a.   cluster sampling
    b.   stratified sampling
    c.   purposive sampling
    d.   simple random sampling

_____ 9.   If you were to obtain a systematic sample of 40 from a population of 600, and your randomly selected starting point is 12, your next three selections should be:
    a.   42, 92, 137
    b.   27, 42, 57
    c.   90, 140, 190
    d.   24, 36, 48

_____ 10.   The reason for the *Literary Digest*'s incorrect prediction of the outcome of the 1936 presidential election was that:
     a.   a significant percentage of voters changed their minds between the time of the poll and Election Day
     b.   the sample was too small
     c.   the *Literary Digest* used mailed questionnaires rather than the more accurate personal interview method
     d.   the sampling frame systematically excluded the poor, thereby producing an unrepresentative sample

_____ 11.   Which type of sampling is most dependent for its effectiveness on the adequacy of a sampling frame?
     a.   simple random sampling
     b.   quota sampling
     c.   purposive sampling
     d.   cluster sampling

_____ 12.   Which of the following nonprobability sampling methods most closely resembles stratified random sampling?
     a.   quota sampling
     b.   convenience sampling
     c.   purposive sampling
     d.   cluster sampling

_____ 13.   Suppose you wanted to survey registered voters in Anytown, U.S.A., on the question of U.S. military involvement in Central America. An important aspect of your research is to see if ethnic background is related to differences in attitudes toward the role of the U.S. in Central America. A list of the 2,000 registered voters in Anytown shows that 1,650 are white, 300 are black, and 50 are Hispanic. Which of the following sampling methods would be the BEST to use in this situation?
     a.   cluster sampling
     b.   simple random sampling
     c.   proportionate stratified sampling
     d.   disproportionate stratified sampling

_____ 14.   In survey research, the size of a sample should:
  a.   always be as large as possible, because any increase in sample size improves the accuracy of the results
  b.   not be any larger than 2,000
  c.   be no less than 5 percent of the population
  d.   be estimated by deciding how much sampling error the researcher is willing to tolerate

_____ 15.   Suppose you are doing a study of cheating among seniors at your college in which 38 percent of the seniors in your sample reported having cheated at least once during college. If you calculated a standard error of 4, what would be the 95 percent confidence interval?
  a.   34–42
  b.   30–46
  c.   26–50
  d.   36–40

True-False   Circle T is the answer is true, F if it is false.

T   F   1.   The major aim of sampling is to provide accurate estimates of unknown population parameters from sample statistics.

T   F   2.   Samples can be accurate whether or not the sampling frame is complete.

T   F   3.   The *Literary Digest*'s inaccurate prediction of the 1936 election stemmed from use of the wrong type of sampling design.

T   F   4.   A vacant lot contained in a listing of dwelling places in a city would be a blank foreign element.

T   F   5.   Probability and nonprobability sampling designs are equally capable of producing representative samples.

T   F   6.   Nonprobability samples are often used because of their convenience and economy.

T   F   7.   The major difference between simple random samples and systematic samples is that the latter are not selected randomly.

T   F   8.   The incorrect poll predictions of the 1948 presidential elections resulted from drawbacks in the use of cluster sampling.

T   F   9.   Stratified sampling is used to ensure that certain groups are adequately represented in a sample.

T   F   10.   Clusters to be used in cluster sampling must always be natural aggregates, such as city blocks, schools, or churches.

T   F   11.   The larger the sample, the more accurate its estimates will be.

T   F   12.   The standard error is calculated by dividing the standard deviation of the sample by the square root of the sample size.

T   F   13.   One must calculate the standard error in order to calculate the confidence interval.

T   F   14.   If the mean age in a sample is 23 and the standard error of the mean is 2, we can be 95 percent confident that the population mean falls in the range 21 to 25.

T   F   15.   Nonresponse error is a part of sampling error.

EXERCISES AND PROJECTS

Exercise 8-1

A professor at a small midwestern college wishes to study the starting salaries of last year's class of 60 business administration and liberal arts majors. The data presented in the table below are to be used to complete Exercises 8-1, 8-2, and 8-3.

	Name	Starting Salary (in thousands of dollars)	Major
1.	Adkins	13.5	L (liberal arts)
2.	Appleby	15.5	B (business administration)
3.	Baldwin	17	B
4.	Bennett	16	B
5.	Brummett	14	L

	Name	Starting Salary (in thousands of dollars)	Major
6.	Bullock	24	B
7.	Carreway	14.5	L
8.	Clements	21.5	B
9.	Cooke	16.0	B
10.	Davis	16.5	B
11.	Dellinger	17	L
12.	Dent	14.5	L
13.	Derrick	18	B
14.	Ellis	21	B
15.	Farr	16	L
16.	Foster	15	L
17.	Furman	13	L
18.	Garrett	15	B
19.	Gehrig	15.5	L
20.	Giles	9.5	L
21.	Harris	15	B
22.	Hayes	14.5	B
23.	Higgs	13	B
24.	Hooper	20	B
25.	Jervis	15	L
26.	Johnson	13.5	B
27.	Jones	11	L
28.	Kendrick	14	L
29.	Knott	14	L
30.	Lambert	18	B
31.	Ledbetter	19	B
32.	Lovedahl	12	B
33.	McCall	14	B
34.	Madison	15	B
35.	Massey	14.5	B
36.	Medlock	13	L
37.	Moran	12	L
38.	Mullins	15.5	B
39.	Newell	16.5	B
40.	Newton	15	B
41.	O'Brien	14	B
42.	Paschal	14	L
43.	Petway	17.5	B

	Name	Starting Salary (in thousands of dollars)	Major
44.	Pruitt	15.5	B
45.	Ragsdale	21	B
46.	Retton	13.5	L
47.	Rogers	14	B
48.	Sharpe	14.5	B
49.	Smith	20	L
50.	Sprouse	14.5	L
51.	Stillwell	15	L
52.	Taylor	16.5	B
53.	Thompson	12.5	B
54.	Tucker	15	L
55.	Underwood	15.5	B
56.	Vance	13	B
57.	Waddell	16	B
58.	Whitlock	13	L
59.	Wood	16	B
60.	Young	15.5	L

Mean starting salary: $15,400

Business administration majors: 36

Liberal arts majors: 24

a. Using simple random sampling, select a sample of 10 persons. List the names of the persons you selected.

1. _____

2. _____

3. _____

4. _____

5. _____

6. _____

7. _____

8. _____

9. _____

10. _____

b. Calculate the mean starting salary for your sample of 10 graduates.
    Mean starting salary: _____

c. Using the mean you calculated for the sample above, calculate the mean
    starting salary for the population of 60 graduates.
    Estimated starting salary: _____

d. Compare your estimated mean salary with the actual figure given at the
    bottom of the list of graduates. The difference between the actual mean
    salary and your estimate is the result of sampling error (assuming that
    you made no arithmetic errors).
    Sampling error = _____

e. What might you do to decrease the sampling error in this task?

Exercise 8-2

Using the list of graduates provided, select a systematic sample of 15 graduates. To
begin, you must calculate your sampling interval (k) and then select a random number
to start with. Indicate what these are in the spaces provided, then list the names of the
15 graduates selected for your sample.

a. Sampling interval (k) = _____
b. Start = _____
c. Graduates selected:
    1. _____
    2. _____
    3. _____
    4. _____
    5. _____
    6. _____
    7. _____
    8. _____
    9. _____
    10. _____
    11. _____
    12. _____
    13. _____
    14. _____
    15. _____
d. Calculate the mean starting salary of the sample.
    Mean starting salary = _____

e.   Use this statistic to estimate the mean starting salary of the total number of graduates.
Estimated mean salary: _____

f.   Compare this estimate with the actual starting salary given earlier to determine how much sampling error you have in this sample.
Sampling error = _____

g.   What might be done to decrease the amount of sampling error?

Exercise 8-3

Using the list of graduates provided, select a stratified sample of 15 graduates. The graduates are to be stratified by major (B = business administration, L = liberal arts).

a.   List below the names of the business administration majors you selected.
1.   _____
2.   _____
3.   _____
4.   _____
5.   _____
6.   _____
7.   _____
8.   _____
9.   _____
10.   _____
11.   _____
12.   _____
13.   _____
14.   _____
15.   _____

b.   List below the names of the liberal arts majors you selected.
1.   _____
2.   _____
3.   _____
4.   _____
5.   _____
6.   _____
7.   _____
8.   _____

9. _____
10. _____
11. _____
12. _____
13. _____
14. _____
15. _____

c. Calculate the mean starting salary of your sample: _____

d. Estimate the starting salary for the population of graduates based on the sample mean.
    Estimated starting salary: _____

e. Compare the estimated starting salary with the actual starting salary to determine your sampling error:_____ Sampling error = _____

f. Compare your sampling error in this sample with the error in an equal size sample (such as that selected for Exercise 8-2). How do they differ?

    Why do you suppose they differ?

Exercise 8-4

You want a sample of driver's license holders in Mellowberg, California, and the California Department of Motor Vehicles agrees to provide this sample data from a data tape that lists all current license holders. You want to estimate the number of years people have had their licenses. The standard deviation of this value in a population is .15, and you want the standard error of your estimate to be no larger than .012. Assuming there are 8,000 driver's license holders in Mellowberg, how big should your sample be?

CHAPTER 9

OBSERVATIONAL METHODS

CHAPTER ABSTRACT

In this chapter, we first discuss the four forms of data collection used in the social sciences and exemplify the idea of triangulation--the practice of using more than one form to test a hypothesis. Next we discuss the various reasons for and ways of using observation in social science research. We then discuss the types of behavior that researchers observe and present strategies for conducting direct observations and recording data. The chapter concludes with a discussion of controlled observation in the laboratory and the field.

CHAPTER OBJECTIVES

After studying this chapter, you should be able to:

1. discuss the idea of triangulation.

2. discuss the roles of observation.

3. name the types of behavior and research purposes to which observation can be applied with satisfactory results.

4. describe the timing and recording of observations.

5. explain the meaning of inference in the course of observation.

6. describe the major types of observation.

7. discuss the strengths and weaknesses of the laboratory experiment as a type of observation, and distinguish between experimental and mundane realism.

8. cite the major sources of bias in laboratory experiments.

9. define field experiments and compare and contrast this technique with laboratory experimentation.

MAIN POINTS

Introduction

There are four general forms of data collection: observational methods, survey research, secondary data analysis, and qualitative research.

Triangulation

Data in the social sciences are obtained in either formal or informal settings and involve either verbal (oral or written) or nonverbal acts or responses. A variety of combinations of these two settings for data collection and the two types of acts led to the development of the four major forms of data collection just alluded to. To a certain degree, research findings are affected by the nature of the data collection method used. Findings that are very strongly affected by the method used could be artifacts rather than objective facts. In order to minimize the risk of erroneous conclusions, two or more methods of data collection can be used. This is the essence of triangulation: when possible, hypotheses should be tested and variables should be measured with two or more data collection methods.

Roles of Observation

Modern social science is rooted in observation, and this technique of studying behavior has a number of distinguishing characteristics and/or advantages: 1) it is direct; 2) it takes place in natural settings; 3) it allows the study of people who cannot or will not report their own behavior; 4) it invites comparison of verbal reports and actual behavior; and 5) it facilitates analysis of the context in which behavior occurs. Whatever the purpose of the study and the observational procedure utilized, three major considerations are to be dealt with if the obtained data are to be systematic and meaningful: what to observe, when to observe and how to record, and how much inference is required.

Types of Behavior

The first significant consideration concerns a decision on what should be observed. Observation is particularly well suited for studying nonverbal, spatial, extralinguistic, and linguistic behavior. A second consideration in observational studies concerns the timing and recording of observations. Researchers using observation must develop techniques to sample time periods. Observation requires the development of systems to categorize behavior; these systems may be inductive, deductive, or both. They must comprise a set of explicit, exhaustive, and mutually exclusive categories.

Inference in the Course of Observation

A third consideration in structured observational studies relates to the degree of inference required by the observer. The greater the inference, the greater the reliability problem, and the greater the need to train the observers in the use of observation systems.

Types of Observation and Controlled Observations

The extent to which decisions regarding the types of behavior, timing and recording, and degree of inference are systematically and rigorously implemented is a criterion by which we can distinguish between controlled and noncontrolled observational systems. Controlled observational systems are typified by clear and explicit decisions on what, how, and when to observe; a noncontrolled system is considerably less systematic and allows great flexibility. Controlled observations are carried out either in the laboratory or in the field.

Laboratory Experimentation

The most controlled method of data collection in the social sciences is laboratory experimentation; it involves the introduction of conditions in a controlled environment (laboratory) that simulate certain features of a natural environment. There is a distinction to be made between two senses in which any given experiment can be said to be realistic. In one sense, an experiment is realistic if the situation is realistic to the research participants: if it involves and has an impact on them. This kind of realism is commonly termed experimental realism. The second sense of realism refers to the extent to which events occurring in a laboratory setting are likely to occur in the "real world," and this type is known as mundane realism.

There are three sources of bias in laboratory experiments: 1) bias due to the demand characteristics of the experimental situation itself (when respondents are aware that they are being observed and that certain responses are expected from them); 2) bias due to the unintentional influence of the experimenters (when experimenters know what effects they desire from individuals, they may unintentionally communicate their expectations in various ways); 3) measurement artifacts (when the process of measuring sensitizes participants or when measurements are imprecise or made at the wrong time).

Field Experiments

A field experiment is a research study in a natural situation in which one or more independent variables are manipulated by investigators under as carefully controlled conditions as the situation permits. The main weakness of field experiments is limited control of intrinsic and especially of extrinsic factors. This problem is somewhat offset by field experimentation's advantages with respect to experimental and mundane realism.

KEY TERMS (page reference in parenthesis)
To assist you in familiarizing yourself with the Key Terms, imagine a series of "short answer" questions that ask you to define each term in your own words, using the text's discussion as a guide.

controlled observation (196)   mundane realism (198)
demand characteristics (198)   noncontrolled observation (196)
experimental realism (198)   nonverbal behavior (191)
experimenter bias (199)   spatial behavior (193)
extralinguistic behavior (193)   time-sampling (193-194)
field experimentation (201)   triangulation (188)
linguistic behavior (192)

SELF-EVALUATION EXERCISES

Introduction

1.   Ultimately, all social research rests on some sort of _____.
2.   In addition to observation, three other general forms of data collection may be distinguished. These are _____, _____, and _____.

Triangulation

3.   Data in the social sciences are obtained with either _____ or _____ settings and involve either _____ or _____ acts or responses.
4.   Triangulation involves _____.

Roles of Observation

5.   The main advantage in observation is its _____.
6.   Observation is useful for describing phenomena as they occur in their ____
     _____.

7.   Three major considerations of research involving observation are:
     1.   _____
     2.   _____
     3.   _____

Types of Behavior

8.   The "body movements of the organism" constitute what is known as _____
     _____.

9.   Spatial behavior refers to _____.
10. If we were to observe how loudly members of a local school board speak during
     board meetings, we would be observing _____.

Timing and Recording

11. Time-sampling schedules are used to ensure that observations are _____
     _____.

12. Time-sampling schedules are often not useful for obscuring events that occur
     _____.

13. When a system for accurately recording observations is devised on the basis of
     conceptual definitions, this is called the _____ approach.

14. The _____ approach to recording observations starts with a
     number of observations and then tries to discern enough of a pattern to devise a
     recording scheme.

15. In any system for accurately recording observations, the categories must be
     _____, _____, and _____.

Inference in the Course of Observation

16. Provide some examples of behaviors that would require a low level of inference
     on the part of the observer.

     _____

     _____

     _____

     _____

17.   Provide some examples of behaviors that would require a high level of inference on the part of the observer.

_____

_____

_____

_____

Types of Observations and Controlled Observations

18.   Social scientists often distinguish between two types of observation: _____ and _____.

19.   Controlled observations may be carried out in the _____ or in the _____.

Laboratory Experimentation

20.   Laboratory experiments possess two major advantages over other methods of observation:

   1.   _____

   2.   _____

21.   If the participants in a laboratory experiment regard the situation as realistic, then the experiment is said to possess _____.

22.   In a laboratory experiment, bias due to demand characteristics can occur when:

_____

_____

_____.

23.   A common method of reducing experimenter bias is the use of _____

_____.

24.   Behavior on the part of an experimenter that is not supposed to affect the experiment, but that nevertheless influences participants, results in

_____.

25.   How can experimenter bias be prevented in an experiment?

_____

_____

_____

26.   While the use of cameras and other kinds of recording devices may reduce bias in laboratory experiments due to _____, they may increase the likelihood of bias due to _____.

27.   The difficulties in controlling _____ factors are substantially greater in field experiments than in laboratory experiments.

Field Experiments

28. The main advantage that field experiments have over laboratory experiments is that:

_____

_____.

29. The main weakness of field experiments is:

_____

_____.

REVIEW TESTS

Multiple-Choice   Place the letter corresponding to the one BEST answer in the space provided.

_____ 1. Suppose we were to observe the facial expressions of members of a jury when the defendant is brought into the courtroom. This behavior would fall into the category of:
   a. linguistic behavior
   b. extralinguistic behavior
   c. nonverbal behavior
   d. spatial behavior

_____ 2. Suppose we were to observe the movements of persons in a room in which there is another person who appears to have a physical handicap. This behavior would fall into the category of:
   a. linguistic behavior
   b. extralinguistic behavior
   c. nonverbal behavior
   d. spatial behavior

_____ 3. As a method of data collection, direct observation is more useful than verbal reports in all of the following EXCEPT:
   a. studying behavior as it occurs in natural settings
   b. studying behavior as it actually occurs
   c. studying persons who are able and willing to articulate themselves meaningfully and clearly
   d. studying the contextual background of behavior

_____ 4. The time-sampling schedule is used:
    a.   to determine the context of observation
    b.   to judge the accuracy of inferences drawn from observations
    c.   to ensure that observations are representative of a defined population of ongoing occurrences
    d.   especially when the researcher's purpose is to observe behavior that occurs infrequently

_____ 5. Bales's system called Interaction Process Analysis:
    a.   studies spatial behavior
    b.   assumes a representative sample of behavior
    c.   avoids the artificiality of interviewer and respondent roles
    d.   assumes a good study design

_____ 6. The LEAST controlled method of observation is:
    a.   the laboratory experiment
    b.   the field experiment
    c.   spatial observation
    d.   the case study

_____ 7. A major advantage of laboratory experiments is that they:
    a.   examine behavior in a natural setting
    b.   provide unambiguous evidence of causality
    c.   allow observations to be influenced by extrinsic factors
    d.   avoid the artificiality of interviewer and respondent roles

_____ 8. If a person volunteers for an experiment entitled "Cooperation and Competition," and then tries to be extremely cooperative because she expects the hypothesis will confirm that females are more cooperative than males, this would produce biased results because of:
    a.   experimenter bias
    b.   demand characteristics
    c.   participant bias
    d.   measurement artifacts

_____ 9.   If participants in a laboratory experiment are aware that their behavior is being recorded by camera, there could be a problem of:
        a.   demand characteristics
        b.   experimenter bias
        c.   measurement artifacts
        d.   analytic induction

_____ 10.   The main difference between laboratory experiments and field experiments has to do with the:
        a.   setting
        b.   time frame of observation
        c.   accuracy of inferences drawn from observation
        d.   kinds of behavior observed

_____ 11.   An important advantage of the use of triangulation in social research is that it:
        a.   gives researchers a means of applying methods of internal validation
        b.   helps distinguish between experimental realism and mundane realism
        c.   explicitly defines the units of observations
        d.   reduces the biases that stem from single methodologies

_____ 12.   An observational study finds that adolescent blacks interact at greater distance than adolescent whites. This study is most likely to be examining:
        a.   spatial behavior
        b.   extralinguistic behavior
        c.   nonverbal behavior
        d.   linguistic behavior

_____ 13.   A researcher unknowingly influences subjects' responses by nodding at "good" responses and frowning at "bad" responses. The researcher's behavior is an example of:
        a.   a measurement artifact
        b.   mundane realism
        c.   a demand characteristic
        d.   experimenter bias

_____ 14.   Piliavin et al.'s study of altruistic behavior among New York City subway riders is an example of a:

     a.   field experiment

     b.   triangulated study

     c.   case study

     d.   laboratory experiment

_____ 15.   The primary weakness of field experiments is that:

     a.   systematic variations cannot be introduced into existing conditions

     b.   experimental situations are difficult to construct within the framework of the experiment

     c.   intrinsic and extrinsic sources of validity are difficult to control for

     d.   independent variables cannot be manipulated directly

True-False   Circle T is the answer is true, F if it is false.

T   F   1.   Triangulation involves using one method of data collection to test three hypotheses.

T   F   2.   Participant observation is the most appropriate form of data collection when the focus is on nonverbal actions in informed settings.

T   F   3.   Direct observation is recommended in research settings in which persons being studied have difficulty verbally communicating their thoughts.

T   F   4.   All forms of observation require that the persons being studied should be unaware that they are being observed.

T   F   5.   Observing where members of a group set themselves in relation to the leader of the group involves the study of spatial behavior.

T   F   6.   The time-sampling schedule would be appropriate to use in studies of how people react to presidential assassinations.

T   F   7.   The most controlled method of data collection in the social sciences is the field experiment.

T   F   8.   Television cameras and other devices for recording observations are sometimes used to eliminate bias in laboratory experiments resulting from measurement artifacts.

T   F   9.   Field experiments generally encounter greater difficulty than do laboratory experiments in controlling intrinsic and extrinsic factors.

T   F   10.   Procedures for recording observations in field experiments are similar to those in laboratory experiments.

EXERCISES AND PROJECTS

Exercise 9-1

The concept of triangulation is illustrated by the discrepancy some researchers have found between what people actually do and what they say they do. For example, a survey questionnaire might show that 70 percent of a country's eligible voters cast ballots in the last election, whereas the county board of elections might put the actual voter turnout at only 50 percent.

Show how the principle of triangulation could be applied in measuring:

1.   Attitudes toward "law and order"

2.   White attitudes about racial integration in public schools

Project 9-2

For this project, you are to select and read an article from a journal in your major that reports the result of either a laboratory experiment or a field experiment. Your instructor will suggest journals that are likely to contain reports of experimental studies. The purpose of this project is for you to obtain some experience in evaluating experiments.

1.   Give the complete bibliographic reference for the article you selected.

2.   On the basis of the authors' report of how the experiment was carried out, would you say that it had:

    a.   Experimental realism? Why or why not?

    b.   Mundane realism? Why or why not?

3.   If the experiment was lacking in either experimental realism or mundane realism, suggest how it might have been altered to increase the realism.

4.   Is it likely that the experimental results have been contaminated by any of the following? If so, tell how; if not, tell how they were avoided.

    a.   Demand characteristics

    b.   Experimenter bias

    c.   Measurement artifacts

CHAPTER 10

SURVEY RESEARCH

CHAPTER ABSTRACT

In this chapter, we discuss the advantages and disadvantages of more traditional survey methods, explore the activities involved in conducting the three different types of surveys, and conclude by comparing the three methods.

CHAPTER OBJECTIVES

After studying this chapter, you should be able to:

1.   describe the major methods of survey research.

2.   discuss the advantages and disadvantages of mail questionnaires, personal interviews, and telephone interviews.

3.   describe the different types of personal interviews.

4.   describe the basic principles of interviewing.

5.   compare and contrast the relative strengths and weaknesses of the three major methods of data collection involved in survey research.

MAIN POINTS

Introduction

Survey research is an extremely useful approach to studying human behavior that is difficult to observe directly. There are three major methods used to elicit information from respondents: the mail questionnaire, the personal interview, and the telephone interview.

Mail Questionnaire

The mail questionnaire is regarded as an impersonal survey method, and under certain conditions and for a number of research purposes, this technique is useful. Advantages include: lower cost, reduction in biasing error, greater anonymity, considered answers and consultations, and accessibility. Disadvantages include: simple questions are required, no opportunity for probe, no control over who completes the questionnaire, and a low response rate.

The difficulty of securing an acceptable response rate to mail questionnaires requires the use of various strategies that can be adopted to increase the rate of response, including sponsorship, inducements to respond, questionnaire formats and methods of mailing, cover letters, types of mailings, timing of mailings, follow-up procedures like the total design method, and selection of respondents. The question of what constitutes an acceptable response rate cannot be easily answered.

Personal Interview

The personal interview is a face-to-face interpersonal role situation in which an interviewer asks respondents questions designed to obtain answers pertinent to the research hypotheses. The most structured form of interview is schedule-structured, in which the questions, their wording, and their sequence are fixed and are identical for every respondent. The second basic form is the focused or nonscheduled- structured interview, which takes place with respondents known to have been involved in a particular experience, refers to situations that have been analyzed prior to the interview, proceeds on the basis of an interview guide specifying topics related to the research hypotheses, and is focused on the subjective experiences regarding the situations under study. The least structured form of interviewing is the nonstructured or nondirective interview, where no prespecified set of questions is employed, the questions are not asked in a specified order, and no schedule is used.

Personal interviews are extremely effective when dealing with heterogeneous populations and when detailed information is required. Furthermore, they provide good control of the interview situation.

Personal Interview Versus Mail Questionnaire

Personal interviews offer certain advantages over mail questionnaires: greater flexibility, control of the interview situation, high response rate, and collection of supplementary information. On the other hand, personal interviews display three disadvantages: higher cost, interviewer bias, and lack of anonymity.

Principles of Interviewing

The first step in the interviewing process is getting the respondent to cooperate and provide the desired information. Three factors help in motivating respondents to do this: 1) they need to feel that their interactions with the interviewer will be pleasant and satisfying; 2)they need to see the investigation as being worthwhile; 3) barriers to the interview in the respondents' minds need to be overcome. Probing is a technique used in the interviewing process designed to stimulate discussion and obtain more information. Probes have two major functions: 1) they motivate the respondent to elaborate or clarify an answer or to explain the reasons behind the answer; 2) they help focus the conversation on the specific topic of the interview. In general, the less structured the interview, the more important probing becomes as an instrument for eliciting and encouraging further information.

Telephone Interview

The telephone survey is characterized as a semipersonal method of collecting information. Until recently, this technique was regarded with great skepticism due to the risk of a serious sampling bias--that economically underprivileged people were unlikely to have telephones. Today, over 93 percent of the population have telephones, so this bias is minimized.

A technique known as random-digit dialing permits random sampling in a telephone survey, thus eliminating the problems inherent in using telephone directories (unlisted numbers, disconnected phones, and so on). One of the latest developments in telephone surveys is computer-assisted telephone interviewing. Recently, the telephone interview has become more popular among researchers due to the rising cost of personal interviews.

Telephone interviews are most advantageous in terms of their speed, a high response rate, and applicability to heterogeneous populations.

Comparing the Three Survey Methods

Which survey method to use depends on which criteria are most significant to one's research objective.

KEY TERMS (page reference in parenthesis)
To assist you in familiarizing yourself with the Key Terms, imagine a series of "short answer" questions that ask you to define each term in your own words, using the text's discussion as a guide.

computer-assisted telephone
interviewing (CATI) (223)
focused interview (215)
follow-up (210)
mail questionnaire (206)

nondirective interview (215)
probing (221)
random-digit dialing (RDD) (222)
response rate (207)
schedule-structured interview (213)

SELF-EVALUATION EXERCISES

Introduction

1. Survey research is an efficient method of getting information about behavior that the researcher cannot _____.

2. The three methods of survey research are _____, _____, and _____.

Mail Questionnaire

3. "Questionnaires can be sent through the mail; interviewers cannot." This quote suggests that a major disadvantage of mail questionnaires is _____ _____.

4. The _____ errors that derive from variations among interviewers are not present in mail questionnaires.

5. The most serious problem of mail questionnaires is _____ _____.

6. Why are mail questionnaire response rates regarded as a serious drawback to the method?

   _____
   _____
   _____

7. For each of the following factors affecting mail questionnaire response rate, list the action that would yield the highest response rate.
   1. Sponsorship: _____
      _____

2. Inducement: _____
_____

3. Questionnaire length: _____
_____

4. Cover letter: _____
_____

5. Provisions for return of questionnaire: _____
_____
_____

6. Selection of respondent population: _____
_____
_____

7. Follow-up mailings: _____
_____
_____

8. What factors involved in questionnaire format might affect response rates?
_____
_____

9. In what ways do nonrespondents to mail surveys tend to be unrepresentative of an originally defined population?
_____
_____
_____

10. A standardized set of step-by-step procedures designed to improve mail questionnaires is known as TDM, or _____
_____.

11. What two problems might arise from the use of follow-ups to increase the response rate of mail questionnaires?
   1. _____
   2. _____

Personal Interview

12. The most highly structured form of personal interview is called the _____ interview.

13. The schedule-structured interview ensures that variations in responses can be attributed to differences between _____, not to differences between _____.

14.   How does a nonscheduled interview differ from a schedule-structured interview?

_____

_____

_____

Personal Interview Versus Mail Questionnaire

15.   Identify four advantages of personal interviews over mailed questionnaires.
    1. _____
    2. _____
    3. _____
    4. _____

16.   What are three disadvantages of personal interviews compared to mailed questionnaires?
    1. _____
    2. _____
    3. _____

Principles of Interviewing

17.   What are three factors motivating respondents to cooperate in an interview?
    1. _____
    2. _____
    3. _____

18.   During the interview itself, what five guidelines should be followed in asking questions?
    1. _____
    2. _____
    3. _____
    4. _____
    5. _____

19.   The technique used by an interviewer to stimulate discussion and obtain more information is known as _____.

20.   The two major purposes of probes are:
    1. _____
    2. _____

21.   Generally speaking, in what kinds of interviews is probing important?

_____

Telephone Interview

22.   The telephone interview is characterized as a(n) _____ method of collecting information.
23.   The main reason for reluctance to use telephone interviewing in the past was the high likelihood of _____.
24.   Rather than using a telephone book, researchers can now get random samples for telephone interviewing by using a process known as _____

_____.
25.   Identify three drawbacks of the telephone interview.
  1.   _____
  2.   _____
  3.   _____
26.   Indicate which of three survey methods is preferable if the researcher wishes to:
  1.   Minimize cost: _____
  2.   Maximize speed: _____
  3.   Obtain detailed information: _____
  4.   Maximize response rate: _____
  5.   Contact geographically dispersed populations:_____

  _____
  6.   Control the interview situation:_____

  _____

REVIEW TESTS

Multiple-Choice   Place the letter corresponding to the one BEST answer in the space provided.

_____   1.   Which of the following is NOT a principal advantage of mail surveys?
          a.   increased anonymity
          b.   lack of interviewer-induced biases
          c.   ability to include complex questions
          d.   low cost

_____ 2.   Low response rates are a problem largely because:
        a.   interviews are expensive
        b.   the sample does not correspond to the original definition of the population
        c.   the researcher may have too few cases to analyze
        d.   the cost of administering a study remains high even if the sample turns out to be small

_____ 3.   The most promising way to increase the response rate of a mail survey is to:
        a.   offer inducements such as a small amount of money
        b.   use a short questionnaire (1–2 pages in length)
        c.   use one or more follow-up mailings
        d.   carefully select the respondents

_____ 4.   Which is the most useful method for an exploratory study when little is known about the object of investigation?
        a.   mail questionnaires
        b.   telephone interviews
        c.   schedule-structured personal interviews
        d.   nonscheduled personal interviews

_____ 5.   Which of the following is NOT among the advantages of personal interviews over mailed questionnaires?
        a.   greater flexibility
        b.   better control of the interview situation
        c.   less bias
        d.   better response rate

_____ 6.   In conducting personal interviews, which of the following is recommended?
        a.   The interviewer should approach each and every respondent in the same manner.
        b.   The interview should begin by asking questions about the respondent's age, income, and marital status.
        c.   The interviewer should rephrase questions which respondents seem to have trouble answering.
        d.   After the introduction, the interviewer should tell the respondents how they were chosen to be interviewed.

_____ 7.   During a personal interview, the interviewer should:
  a.   ask questions in the same order in which they appear on the questionnaire
  b.   create a quiz atmosphere to ensure that the respondent takes the interview seriously
  c.   skip over questions which appear to confuse or embarrass the respondent
  d.   challenge the respondent if the respondent appears to give evasive or untruthful answers

_____ 8.   In conducting personal interviews, probing is:
  a.   used to determine the reasons for a respondent's answers to certain questions.
  b.   more important in structured that in nonstructured interviewing methods
  c.   a good way to tell if a respondent is lying
  d.   used to establish rapport with respondents

_____ 9.   Telephone surveys are more attractive now than in the past because:
  a.   more people have telephones
  b.   they are more accurate than other methods of survey research
  c.   they are more economical than other methods of survey research
  d.   they eliminate interviewer-induced bias

_____ 10.   In order to do random-digit dialing, one needs to know:
  a.   the name of the person to be called
  b.   only the last four digits of the phone number of the person to be called
  c.   all working telephone exchanges in the areas to be sampled
  d.   when persons to be called will be at home

_____ 11.   Telephone interviews often produce higher-quality data than personal interviews because:
  a.   respondents are more truthful
  b.   interviewers are less exhausted from walking and driving
  c.   interviewers can be directly monitored by a superior
  d.   respondents are less likely to terminate the interview before it is complete

_____ 12.   The "broken off" interview is a kind of nonresponse associated with:
      a.   personal interviews
      b.   captive audience surveys
      c.   telephone surveys
      d.   mail surveys

_____ 13.   On which of the following factors is the mail questionnaire strongest?
      a.   applicability to geographically dispersed populations
      b.   speed in collecting responses
      c.   control over the environment in which responses are elicited
      d.   response rate

_____ 14.   If your greatest concern is to standardize the environment in which respondents give their answers, which survey research method should you employ?
      a.   telephone interview
      b.   personal interview
      c.   mail questionnaire
      d.   field research

_____ 15.   Which method of obtaining survey information is most effective in obtaining a high response rate?
      a.   personal interview
      b.   mail questionnaire
      c.   telephone interview
      d.   mail survey

_____ 16.   Which method of obtaining survey information is most effective in obtaining detailed information?
      a.   personal interview
      b.   mail questionnaire
      c.   telephone interview
      d.   mail survey

_____ 17.   Suppose you were to survey a sample of respondents to see how many could correctly name the justices of the U.S. Supreme Court. Which survey method would be LEAST appropriate?
    a.   mail questionnaire
    b.   personal interview
    c.   telephone interview
    d.   mail survey

_____ 18.   Each of the following is a guideline suggested by the Survey Research Center for conducting a personal interview EXCEPT:
    a.   Tell the respondent how he or she was chosen.
    b.   Adopt one approach and stay with that approach.
    c.   Tell the respondent what you are doing in a way that will stimulate his or her interest.
    d.   Keep instruction brief.

_____ 19.   In response to one of your interview questions, a respondent simply says "Yes." In order to get more information from the respondent, you should resort to the techniques known as:
    a.   focusing
    b.   redirection
    c.   transference
    d.   probing

_____ 20.   Computer-assisted telephone interviewing (CATI) is likely to be most effective when the researcher is interested in what two factors?
    a.   high response rate and the use of open-ended questions
    b.   randomized questions and a reduction in "broken off" interviews
    c.   more information and greater security
    d.   speed and the use of complex instructions

True-False   Circle T is the answer is true, F if it is false.

T   F   1.   Survey methods are best suited to studying behavior that can be observed directly by the researcher.

T   F   2.   Mail questionnaires require the use of simple questions.

T   F   3.   Other things being equal, a mail questionnaire is more feasible than personal interviewing for studying a nationwide sample.

T   F   4.   Because mail questionnaires are generally anonymous, they tend to have high response rates.

T   F   5.   When conducting personal interviews, the order in which questions are asked is not important as long as questions are asked exactly as they are worded on the questionnaire.

T   F   6.   The schedule-structured interview requires the least expertise on the part of the interviewer.

T   F   7.   The more structured an interview is, the more important probing becomes.

T   F   8.   The nonscheduled interview is structured only to the extent that a particular topic is the basis of the encounter between the interviewer and the subject.

T   F   9.   The telephone interview produces a higher response rate than either mail questionnaires or personal interviews.

T   F   10.   Telephone interviewing is an especially useful alternative to the personal interview when the interview is a relatively simple one.

EXERCISES AND PROJECTS

Project 10-1

The purpose of this project, which can be done either individually or in a group, is to give you some practical experience in the application of the three survey research methods: mail questionnaires, personal interviews, and telephone interviews.

A simple survey instrument is provided, designed to measure the attitudes of college students toward cheating. Make 20 copies of this survey (more if you or your professor's department can afford it) and obtain responses from 10 students using personal interviews and from 10 other students using telephone interviews. (Note that the survey is designed such that the words you are to say during the interview are in capital letters). Next, obtain responses from an additional 10 students by means of mail questionnaires. Some modification of the survey instrument will be required to make it suitable for mailing. To avoid additional cost, it is recommended that you use campus mail.

When the responses have been collected, evaluate each of the survey research methods in terms of the following criteria.

Response rate

Control over interview situation

Speed in obtaining responses

Eliciting truthful responses

In the following space, indicate any particular problems you encountered in the application of the three survey methods. For example, did telephoning result in any "broken off" interviews? During personal interviews, how much trouble did you have establishing rapport with respondents? Did respondents appear to be evasive or reluctant to respond?

Survey Attitudes Toward Cheating (sample instrument)

HELLO, MY NAME IS _____ AND I'M CONDUCTING A SHORT SURVEY FOR MY RESEARCH METHODS COURSE ON THE ATTITUDES OF COLLEGE STUDENTS TOWARD CHEATING. COULD I ASK YOU JUST A FEW QUESTIONS ON THE SUBJECT? IT WILL TAKE ONLY A MINUTE OR TWO.

1.   WHAT IS YOUR CLASS RANK? ( ) freshman ( ) sophomore
( ) junior   ( ) senior

NOW, I'M GOING TO READ YOU SOME STATEMENTS, AND I WOULD LIKE YOU TO TELL ME WHETHER YOU STRONGLY AGREE, MILDLY AGREE, MILDLY DISAGREE, OR STRONGLY DISAGREE WITH EACH STATEMENT.

Circle one:

2.   WITH SO MUCH PRESSURE ON COLLEGE STUDENTS TO GET GOOD GRADES, CHEATING IS INEVITABLE. SA   MA   MD   SD

3.   TO GET AHEAD IN COLLEGE, OR IN LIFE IN GENERAL, YOU SOMETIMES HAVE TO DO THINGS THAT AREN'T VERY HONEST.
SA   MA   MD   SD

4.   THE PERSON WHO SEES SOMEONE CHEAT BUT DOES NOT TURN THAT PERSON IN IS JUST AS DISHONEST AS THE CHEATER.
SA   MA   MD   SD

5.   SUPPOSE YOU SAW SOMEONE CHEAT ON A TEST IN ONE OF YOUR CLASSES. HOW LIKELY WOULD IT BE THAT YOU WOULD TURN THAT PERSON IN TO YOUR PROFESSOR?

Check one: ( ) very likely
( ) somewhat likely
( ) somewhat unlikely
( ) very unlikely

6.   SUPPOSE YOU AND YOUR BEST FRIEND ARE TAKING A COURSE WHICH YOUR FRIEND WILL FAIL IF HE OR SHE DOES NOT PASS THE FINAL

EXAM. HOW LIKELY WOULD IT BE THAT YOU LET YOUR FRIEND COPY ANSWERS FROM YOUR EXAM?

Check one:
                 ( ) very likely
                 ( ) somewhat likely
                 ( ) somewhat unlikely
                 ( ) very unlikely

7.   HAVE YOU EVER CHEATED IN COLLEGE?

            ( ) yes   ( ) no

THAT COMPLETES THE SURVEY. THANK YOU FOR YOUR COOPERATION.

Project 10-2

Locate at least two articles in social science journals that report survey results based on the use of mail questionnaires. (*Public Opinion Quarterly* would be a good source.) For each of the articles, provide complete bibliographic information and answer the following:

1.   What was the topic or focus of the study?

2.   What was the return rate?

3.   What was the population that was sampled?

4.   What was the length of the questionnaire?

5.   How complex were the questions?

6.   What kinds of return mail provisions were employed?

7.   What methods, if any, were used to increase the initial return rate?

CHAPTER 11

QUESTIONNAIRE CONSTRUCTION

CHAPTER ABSTRACT

In this chapter, we focus on the questionnaire as the main instrument in survey research. We start by discussing the foundation of all questionnaires--the question. We then look at the content of questions; differentiate between open-ended, closed-ended, and contingency-type questions; and analyze their format and sequencing. Next, we explore possible biases in the wording of questions, as well as leading, double-barreled, and threatening questions. Finally, we give important pointers on the cover letter accompanying the questionnaire and the instructions included in it.

CHAPTER OBJECTIVES

After studying this chapter, you should be able to:

1.   cite the major considerations involved in formulating questions: content, structure, format, and sequence.

2.   discuss the ways in which questions can be utilized to elicit factual information, opinions, and attitudes from respondents.

3.   distinguish among and discuss the three types of question structures: open-ended, close-ended, and contingency.

4.   describe the various formats utilized to ask questions for different research purposes.

5.   explain the importance of question sequencing in a questionnaire.

6.   identify the pitfalls in questionnaire construction.

7.   describe the characteristics of the cover letter and relevant instructions for questionnaire completion by respondents.

MAIN POINTS

The Question

The foundation of all questionnaires is the question. The major considerations involved in formulating questions are content, structure, format, and sequence.

Content of Questions

Most questions can be classified into two general categories. Factual questions are designed to elicit objective information from respondents regarding their background, their environment, their habits, and so forth. The most common type of factual question is the background question. Opinion questions explore respondents' opinions (specific expressions of underlying attitudes) and attitudes (general orientations). Survey questions about opinions and attitudes present more problems in construction than questions about facts, partly because the former are more sensitive to changes in wording, emphasis, and sequence.

Types of Questions

Three types of question structures can be distinguished. Closed-ended questions offer respondents a set of answers from which they are asked to choose the one that most closely represents their views. These questions are easy to ask and quick to be answered; they require no writing by either respondent or interviewer, and their analysis is straightforward. Their major drawback is that they may introduce bias, either by forcing respondents to choose from given alternatives or by making respondents select alternatives that might not otherwise have occurred to them.

Open-ended questions are not followed by any kind of specified choice, and respondents' answers are recorded in full; they are flexible, have possibilities of depth, enable interviewers to clear up misunderstandings, and encourage rapport. However, they are difficult to answer and still more difficult to analyze.

Contingency questions reflect a special case of closed-ended questions; they apply only to a subgroup of respondents. Relevance of such questions to a particular subgroup is determined by a preceding filter question.

Question Format

There are different techniques for structuring the response categories of closed-ended questions. One of the most common of these formats is the rating scale, used whenever respondents are asked to make a judgment in terms of sets of ordered categories. Such scales measure the intensity of feelings toward something.

The matrix question is a method for organizing a large set of rating questions that have the same response categories. Ranking is used in questionnaires whenever researchers want to obtain information regarding the degree of importance or the priorities that people assign to a set of attitudes or objects.

Sequence of Questions

Two general patterns of question sequence have been found to be most appropriate for motivating respondents to cooperate. In the funnel sequence, each successive question is related to the previous question, and the questions get progressively narrower in scope. In the inverted funnel sequence, narrower questions are followed by broader ones.

Avoiding Bias: Pitfalls in Questionnaire Construction

Questions must be worded so that they are comprehended by respondents. A number of important factors must be taken into consideration:

A response set is the tendency to answer all questions in a specific direction regardless of the question's content. Leading questions are those that are phrased in such a manner that it appears to respondents that the researcher expects a particular answer.

Threatening questions are those that respondents may find embarrassing and therefore difficult to answer. It has been determined that the reporting of certain behaviors decreases as questions increase in their degree of threat.

Double-barreled questions include two or more questions in one, and this poses a problem if respondents feel differently about the issues involved.

Cover Letter

A cover letter must succeed in overcoming any resistance or prejudice that respondents may have against the survey. This document should: 1) identify the sponsoring organization and/or the persons conducting the study; 2) explain the purpose of the study; 3) tell why it is important that respondents answer the questionnaire; and 4) assure respondents that the information provided will be held in strict confidence.

Instructions

Instructions should be included at the beginning of questionnaires and should accompany any questions that are not self-explanatory.

KEY TERMS (page reference in parenthesis)
To assist you in familiarizing yourself with the Key Terms, imagine a series of "short answer" questions that ask you to define each term in your own words, using the text's discussion as a guide.

attitude (231)
closed-ended question (233)
contingency question (235)
double-barreled question (242)
factual question (231)
filter question (235)
leading question (241)
matrix question (237)
open-ended question (233)

opinion (232)
quantifiers (237)
question (230)
ranking (238)
rating (236)
response bias (242)
response set (240)
threatening question (241)

SELF-EVALUATION EXERCISES

The Question

1.   The questionnaire has the dual function of translating the research objectives into specific _____ and _____ the respondent to answer.

Content of Questions

2.   Questions are of two types: (1) _____ questions and (2) _____ questions.
3.   Factual questions are redesigned to elicit _____ information about the respondent.

4.   Give four reasons why respondents provide less than accurate responses to factual questions.

1.   _____

2.   _____

3.   _____

4.   _____

5.   Opinion questions attempt to get verbal expressions of respondents'
_____.

6.   Attitudes are described in terms of their _____, _____, and _____.

7.   Attitudes cannot be adequately measured with a simple opinion item because

_____.

8.   Compared to factual questions, attitude questions are more sensitive to changes in _____, _____, _____, and

_____.

Types of Questions

9.   In terms of structure, the three main types of questions are _____, _____, and _____.

10.   Closed-ended questions have what two advantages over open-ended questions?

1.   _____

2.   _____

11.   What is the main disadvantage of closed-ended questions?

_____

_____

_____

12.   What are two strengths of open-ended questions?

1.   _____

2.   _____

13.   What is a major drawback in the use of open-ended questions?

_____

_____

14.   What are the four objectives mentioned in the text that would favor the use of open-ended questions instead of closed-ended questions?

1.   _____

2.   _____

3.   _____

4.   _____

15.   When are contingency questions called for?

_____

16.   The item preceding a contingency question is called a(n) _____.

Question Format

17.   Of the three formats for allowing respondents to indicate their answers to closed-ended questions (check a box, check a blank, circle a response number), which is preferred for clarity?

_____

Why? _____
Which is least preferred? _____
Why? _____

18.   When respondents are asked to select one of a set of ordered response categories, the question format is called a(n) _____.

19.   In a rating scale, answers reflect the _____ of the respondent's judgment.

20.   Rating scales generally yield measurements at the _____ level.

21.   The matrix format is useful for _____.

22.   When we want to know how respondents give priorities to different things, we may ask them to _____ these things along some dimension.

Sequence of Questions

23.   A question sequence where each successive question is of a narrower scope is known as a _____ sequence.

24.   The funnel sequence is the preferred sequence of questions when the objective of the research is to _____

_____

25.   The inverted funnel sequence is the preferred organization of questions in a questionnaire when _____

_____

26.   Generally speaking, what kinds of questions appear at or near the beginning of a questionnaire?

_____

_____

27.   What kinds of questions should appear later in a questionnaire?

_____

_____

Avoiding Bias: Pitfalls in Questionnaire Construction

28.   In a survey of a general population, questionnaire items should be capable of being understood by a person with at least _____ years of schooling.
29.   The tendency to answer all questions in the same fashion regardless of their content is known as a(n) _____.
30.   The response set is especially likely to be a problem when _____ _____.

31.   What are some ways of avoiding response sets?
_____
_____

32.   A question worded in such a way that it appears that the researcher expects a certain answer is called a(n) _____ question.
33.   What kind of bias is likely to result from asking threatening questions?
_____

34.   What is wrong with asking double-barreled questions?
_____
_____

Cover Letter

35.   Why should a cover letter to a mail questionnaire be more detailed than the introduction to a personal interview?
_____
_____

36.   What four items should a cover letter include?
   1.   _____
   2.   _____
   3.   _____
   4.   _____
37.   Instructions should always be written for questions that are not _____
_____.

REVIEW TESTS

Multiple-Choice   Place the letter corresponding to the one BEST answer in the space provided.

_____ 1.   Questions concerning age, sex, and marital status are classified as _____ questions.
        a.   attitude
        b.   opinion
        c.   factual
        d.   open-ended

_____ 2.   The question "Should the government guarantee a job to anyone who wants one?" is an example of a(n):
        a.   factual question
        b.   attitude question
        c.   opinion question
        d.   double-barreled question

_____ 3.   The items in this review test are examples of:
        a.   closed-ended questions
        b.   open-ended questions
        c.   motivation questions
        d.   opinion questions

_____ 4.   A questionnaire item which allows respondents to answer in their own words is a(n):
        a.   close-ended question
        b.   open-ended question
        c.   contingency question
        d.   matrix question

_____ 5.   In a questionnaire, we start by asking respondents if they agree that people, regardless of their race or color, should have the same opportunities in life as anyone else. We then proceed to ask questions about whether blacks and whites should go to separate schools, whether the government should require companies to use racial quotas in hiring, and whether respondents would be willing to sell their homes to blacks. This approach would be using the question sequence known as the:
        a.   funnel sequence
        b.   inverted funnel sequence
        c.   longitudinal sequence
        d.   contingency sequence

_____ 6.   In questionnaires, a major drawback in the use of open-ended questions is that they:
      a.   do not enable the researcher to ascertain lack of information or knowledge on the part of the respondent
      b.   prevent the researcher from learning about the process or reasoning by which the respondent arrived at a particular opinion
      c.   call for responses that are often hard to interpret and analyze
      d.   are generally more difficult to word than closed-ended questions

_____ 7.   In constructing questions that prevent respondents from answering items that are irrelevant to them, one should use:
      a.   double-barreled questions
      b.   contingency questions
      c.   funnel-sequence questions
      d.   actual questions

_____ 8.   One virtue of using closed-ended questions is that they:
      a.   are more useful than open-ended questions in situations where respondents do not have firm opinions on a subject or issue
      b.   are more flexible than open-ended questions in how they can be worded
      c.   call for responses that are more easily communicated than responses to open-ended questions
      d.   are better able to reveal a person's reasons for his or her opinions than are open-ended questions

_____ 9.   When the topic of a survey does not easily or strongly motivate respondents to respond, one should use:
      a.   the funnel sequence of questions
      b.   a schedule-structured interview
      c.   the inverted funnel sequence of questions
      d.   matrix questions

_____ 10.   In a questionnaire we find the following sequence:

        15.   Are you married?
            ( ) yes. If yes, answer question 16.
            ( ) no. If no, skip to question 17.

This question is called a:
- a.   filter question
- b.   matrix question
- c.   funnel question
- d.   contingency question

_____ 11.   Which of the following statements concerning questionnaire construction is correct?
- a.   Try to keep the questionnaire short by putting as many questions as you can on as few pages as possible.
- b.   In order to make the most economical use of space, use abbreviations whenever possible.
- c.   Place questions that may be personally embarrassing to respondents at the beginning of the questionnaire so they can be gotten out of the way as soon as possible.
- d.   none of the above

_____ 12.   Which of the following is NOT a potential source of bias in questionnaires?
- a.   inverted funnel sequencing
- b.   question wording
- c.   response sets
- d.   position of questions

_____ 13.   If a researcher suspects that respondents may be answering all questions in a questionnaire in the same way regardless of the content of the questions, there may be a bias due to:
- a.   leading questions
- b.   response sets
- c.   interviewer bias
- d.   double-barreled questions

_____ 14.   A cover letter should do all of the following EXCEPT:
  a.   identify the sponsor of the study
  b.   be less detailed than an interviewer's introductory
          statement
  c.   tell why it is important for the respondent to respond
  d.   explain the purpose of the study

True-False   Circle T if the answer is true, F if it is false.

T   F   1.   "Is police protection in your neighborhood adequate?" is an
                   example of a factual question.

T   F   2.   Attitudes cannot be measured with a single question.

T   F   3.   This true-false question is closed-ended.

T   F   4.   Responses to open-ended questions are generally easier to analyze
                   than responses to closed-ended questions.

T   F   5.   The great value of open-ended questions is that they allow
                   flexibility for probing and clarifying.

T   F   6.   The order in which questions appear in a questionnaire is not
                   particularly important.

T   F   7.   Respondents are more likely to choose, or rank highly, items that
                   appear near the top of a list.

T   F   8.   Initial questions should be difficult to answer so that the
                   respondent will immediately realize what the interview is going to
                   be like.

T   F   9.   The major problem with threatening questions is that respondents
                   will probably not respond to them.

T   F   10.   Research indicates that a form cover letter actually produces a
                   higher response rate than a semipersonal letter.

EXERCISES AND PROJECTS

Exercise 11-1

Identify the error or potential source of bias in the following questions and statements.

1. "Do you agree or disagree with the statement by Pope John Paul II that governments should spend more money on programs to aid the poor?"

2. "Most of the candidates who are running for president are egocentric."
   Check one answer:
   ( ) strongly agree ( ) agree ( ) disagree ( ) strongly disagree

3. "Do you approve or disapprove of recent Supreme Court rulings that suppress the right of children to pray in public schools?"

4. "Do you feel that government workers are corrupt and are paid too much?"

5. "Do you approve or disapprove of the current federal regulations for the disposal of nuclear waste?"

6. "About how many times a day do you think about sex?"

7. "The President is doing a poor job of running the government because he has incompetent advisors." Check whether you:
   ( ) strongly agree ( ) agree ( ) disagree ( ) strongly disagree

Exercise 11-2

For each of the following topics, construct two factual questions and two opinion/attitude questions. Assume that your respondents are college students.

1. *Television viewing preferences*
   Factual 1:
   Factual 2:
   Opinion 1:
   Opinion 2:

2.   *The role of athletics in higher education*
       Factual 1:
       Factual 2:
       Opinion 1:
       Opinion 2:

3.   *Political attitudes and behavior*
       Factual 1:
       Factual 2:
       Opinion 1:
       Opinion 2:

Exercise 11-3

This is an exercise in writing contingency questions using the "GO TO QUESTION 3" format illustrated in the text. From the respondents, who all work for a certain company, you want to learn how they travel to work: whether they drive alone, car-pool, take public transportation, or "other." For respondents who do not car-pool, you want to know whether they have ever car-pooled to work. If respondents have ever car-pooled to work, or if they are currently car-pooling, find out what they believe are the advantages of car-pooling over driving alone. For respondents who have not car-pooled in the past and are not currently car-pooling, find out what disadvantages they see in car-pooling. Construct a set of contingency questions to elicit this information.

Exercise 11-4

Develop a questionnaire for distribution to students on your campus that includes the following elements. In constructing your questionnaire items, be sure to abide by the guidelines for questionnaire construction discussed in Chapter 11 of the text.

1.   Six factual questions.

2.   Four closed-ended and two open-ended questions on issues of campus life.

3.   Four to six matrix questions dealing with a current national social or political issue.

4.   Three questions illustrating the use of the semantic differential.

CHAPTER 12

QUALITATIVE RESEARCH

CHAPTER ABSTRACT

In this chapter, we focus on field research for qualitative study, concentrating on complete participant and participant-as-observer roles. We discuss how researchers select their topics, identify and gain access to their subjects, establish relationships, and record their observations. We also consider how field researchers develop grounded theory based on their data using the process of analytic induction. Finally, we consider the ethical and political dilemmas of field research.

CHAPTER OBJECTIVES

After studying this chapter, you should be able to:

1. identify the principal differences between qualitative and quantitative research.
2. distinguish between "complete participant" and "participant-as-observer" in terms of participant-observation techniques.
3. list the steps involved in the practice of field research.
4. describe the theory of field research.
5. discuss the ethical and political issues of fieldwork.

MAIN POINTS

Introduction

As a method of data collection and analysis, qualitative research derives from the *Verstehen* tradition described in Chapter 1. Qualitative researchers attempt to understand behavior and institutions by getting to know well the persons involved, their values, rituals, symbols, beliefs, and emotions.

Field Research

Field research is the central strategy of data collection associated with qualitative methodology; fieldwork is characterized by its location and by the manner in which it is conducted.

Participant Observation

The method of data collection most closely associated with contemporary field research is participant observation: the process in which investigators attempt to attain some kind of membership in or close attachment to the group they wish to study. A complete participant role means that the observer is wholly concealed; the research objectives are unknown to the observed, and the researcher attempts to become a member of the group under observation. The complete participant role poses a number of methodological problems, and therefore, contemporary fieldworkers most often assume the participant-as-observer role, wherein the researcher's presence is known to the group under investigation; this role also differs from complete participation in that the research goal is explicitly identified.

The Practice of Field Research

The first step in doing field research is to select a subject for investigation. Then the investigator must select an appropriate research site and obtain access. Once this is accomplished, the central aspect of fieldwork presents itself: establishing relationships with those under observation. Once relationships with members of the group have been established, the participant-observer is regarded as a provisional member of the group.

The social complexity of field research is not limited to gaining access and establishing relationships. Leaving the field is no less problematic; this stage depends upon the agreement reached between the observer and the observed at the entrance phase and on the kind of social relationships that developed during the research process.

In field research, the primary sources of data are what people say and do.

Data analysis in qualitative field research is an ongoing process; observers formulate hypotheses and note important themes throughout their studies. Once researchers have identified actions and statements that support their emerging hypotheses, their next step is to look for negative cases--instances that refute the hypotheses. When analyzing qualitative data, it is useful to look for certain regularities, or patterns, that emerge from the numerous observations made during the fieldwork stage. The culmination of the study is writing the report.

Data analysis can be enhanced by using computers. Software programs can speed up analysis and facilitate the coding process and also simplify the preparation of the final research report.

The Theory of Field Research

The goal of field research is to develop a theory that is "grounded," or close and directly relevant to the particular setting under study. Using the "grounded-theory" approach, the researcher first develops conceptual categories from the data, and then makes new observations in order to clarify and elaborate these categories.

An alternative theoretical approach to field research is the method of analytic induction, in which analysis begins by generating a tentative hypothesis explaining the phenomenon observed, and then an attempt is made to verify the hypothesis by observing a small number of cases.

Blue-Collar Community: An Example of Field Research

Kornblum's investigation of a South Chicago community is an excellent example of a field study employing participant observation as the main method of analysis.

Ethical and Political Issues of Fieldwork

Unlike other methods of social research, fieldwork is characterized by long-term and intimate participation in the daily life of those being studied, and hence it is associated with a number of ethical, legal, and political dilemmas.

There are two kinds of ethical issues associated with fieldwork: the problem of potential deception and the impact the fieldwork may have on the lives of those under study.

KEY TERMS (page reference in parenthesis)
To assist you in familiarizing yourself with the Key Terms, imagine a series of "short answer" questions that ask you to define each term in your own words, using the text's discussion as a guide.

analytic induction (268)   informant (264)
complete participant (258)   negative case (267)
field research (257)   participant-as-observer (260)
grounded theory (268)   participant observation (257)

SELF-EVALUATION EXERCISES

Introduction

1.   Qualitative research and its principal methodology, _____, derives
      from the _____ tradition.

Field Research

2.   Field research is defined as _____.
3.   Field research is distinguished by _____.

Participant Observation

4.   The method of data collection principally used in field research is

      _____.

5.   Distinguish between the roles of researchers as complete participants and as
      participants-as-observers.

      _____

      _____

      _____

6.   The complete participant role poses several methodological problems. These
      include:
      1.   _____
      2.   _____
      3.   _____

The Practice of Field Research

7.   What are the six steps in doing field research?
      1.   _____
      2.   _____
      3.   _____
      4.   _____

5. _____

6. _____

8.   What are the advantages and disadvantages of field researchers having the same characteristics (gender, race, age, etc.) of those of the persons being studied?

_____

_____

_____

9.   Instances that refute the hypotheses are termed _____.

The Theory of Field Research

10.   Explain the method of analytic induction.

_____

_____

_____

Ethical and Political Issues of Field Research

11.   What two kinds of ethical questions does field research raise?

1. _____

_____

2. _____

_____

REVIEW TESTS

Multiple-Choice   Place the letter corresponding to the one BEST answer in the space provided.

_____ 1.   Qualitative research is distinguished from quantitative research by:

a.   its unscientific approach

b.   its neatly ordered sequence of steps

c.   the setting in which its observations are made

d.   its sensitivity to ethical concerns

_____ 2. In conducting field research, which of the following is true?
- a. Hypotheses are formulated and tested much as they are in quantitative research.
- b. Data collection and data analysis are distinct and separate stages of the research process.
- c. Subjects must be unaware of being observed.
- d. Data collection and data analysis are ongoing activities.

_____ 3. One of the major strengths of field research is its:
- a. objectivity
- b. generalizability
- c. rigorous model of scientific proof
- d. flexibility

_____ 4. Contemporary fieldwork, which originated in the social reform movement at the turn of the century, found its academic expression in the:
- a. Chicago School
- b. populist movement
- c. gestalt philosophy
- d. _Verstehen_ theory

_____ 5. The possibility that a field researcher might lose his or her research perspective by "going native" poses the greatest danger when the researcher adopts the role of:
- a. complete participant
- b. observer-as-participant
- c. participant-as-observer
- d. complete observer

_____ 6. Which of the following occurs when the researcher acts in the role of complete participant?
- a. The research focus is explicitly defined.
- b. The identity of the researcher is made known to those being observed.
- c. The identity of the researcher is concealed from those being observed.
- d. The identity of the researcher is made known to those being studied, but the purpose of the study is not made known.

_____ 7.   An important technical element of data analysis in field research is:
      a.   using computers for statistical computations
      b.   establishing files
      c.   selecting an appropriate site for observation
      d.   establishing rapport with subjects

_____ 8.   In field research, the method of analytic induction involves:
      a.   developing a preconceived scheme for coding observations
      b.   attempting to verify a tentative hypothesis by meeting a small number of observations
      c.   exploring cause-effect relationships between precisely measured variables
      d.   transferring recorded observations to computer storage devices for purposes of data analysis

_____ 9.   Unlike the role of field researchers as complete participants, the role of participants-as-observers requires researchers to do all of the following EXCEPT:
      a.   explicitly identify their research goal
      b.   make their presence known to the group being studied
      c.   establish relationships with members of the group who subsequently serve as both informants and respondents
      d.   avoid taking notes on the spot in order to avoid suspicion

_____ 10.   Each of the following is a typical stage in the practice of field research EXCEPT:
      a.   selecting a research topic
      b.   finding reliable informants
      c.   analyzing the data gathered
      d.   establishing a control group

_____ 11.   The selection of an appropriate site at which to conduct field research is determined principally by:
      a.   choice of research topic
      b.   type of methodology used
      c.   type of observations to be made
      d.   expected barriers to communication

_____ 12. An important requirement in the researcher's job of establishing good social relations with the group being observed is:

      a.   "going native" in order to put the group at ease
      b.   recording observations as soon as they are made
      c.   understanding the jargon used by the group
      d.   maintaining social distance from members of the group

_____ 13. Opportunities for distortion and misrepresentation of observations are most likely to occur when:

      a.   the observations are not recorded immediately
      b.   codes and symbols are used to record observations
      c.   the researcher comes into the study with an explicit research goal
      d.   audio devices are used to record observations

_____ 14. A researcher begins the process of analyzing data from a study by developing conceptual categories from the data and then making new observations to clarify and elaborate these categories. Such a strategy is most consistent with the:

      a.   analytic induction method
      b.   grounded-theory approach
      c.   participant-observer model
      d.   categorical role theory

_____ 15. Two ethical issues commonly associated with fieldwork are the problem of potential deception and:

      a.   the misapplication of data to social welfare programs
      b.   misappropriation of research funds for personal use
      c.   lack of an adequate control group to serve as the basis for generalizations
      d.   impact the fieldwork may have on the lives of those being studied

True-False   Circle T if the answer is true, F if it is false.

T   F   1.   Field research is a recent development that has its roots in the student activism of the 1960s.

T   F   2.   Field research is an exclusively data-collecting activity.

T   F   3.   The consensus of social scientists is that it is unethical for field researchers to adopt the role of complete participant.

T   F   4.   A strength of field research is its applicability to questions that defy quantification and precise measurement.

T   F   5.   One advantage of the complete participant role is that the researcher can record observations of behavior on the spot.

T   F   6.   When the researcher acts as participant-as-observer, the purpose of the research is known to the persons being studied.

T   F   7.   Kornblum's study, *The Blue-Collar Community*, illustrates the need for the field researcher to make a firm decision about research site at the outset of field research.

T   F   8.   The potential for deception in fieldwork is greatest in studies in which the researcher uses informants.

T   F   9.   With analytic induction, analysis begins with a tentative hypothesis explaining a phenomenon being observed.

T   F   10.   In field research, the primary sources of data are what people say and do.

EXERCISES AND PROJECTS

Project 12-1

Design a field research project in which you would observe the behavior of people in situations in which they are confronted by authority. Choose an appropriate setting such as a traffic court session, a city or county tax office, or a school board meeting.

Spend about an hour observing and recording verbal communications, facial expressions, body movements and interpersonal behavior. Be sure to take careful notes of your observations and prepare a brief report of your findings and conclusions.

Exercise 12-2

Assume that you wish to undertake a field study of a local chapter of Parents Without Partners, an organization for helping people cope with the problem of single parenthood. Write a brief prospectus showing how you would expect to carry out this research. In your prospectus indicate particular problems you might encounter in terms of gaining access to the group, establishing relations with members, recording observations, and analyzing data. What ethical issues might arise in the conduct of your study?

Exercise 12-3

The Internet and the World Wide Web have become an important source of reference and information for social scientists. For example, all of the major representative organizations, such as the American Sociological Association and the American Psychological Association, have sites on the Internet. You can also access a great deal of information concerning research methods on the web. Using the search engine of your choice (Yahoo, Alta Vista, Excite, Lycos, HotBot, GoTo, etc.), plug in a few key words, such as "research methodology," "field research," "participant observation," "quantitative methods," and "qualitative research." The results will be a wealth of additional information that will enhance your understanding of many of the concepts and issues in your research methods class.

CHAPTER 13

SECONDARY DATA ANALYSIS

CHAPTER ABSTRACT

In this chapter, we first discuss the reasons for the increased use of secondary data; then we point out the advantages and inherent limitations of secondary data analysis. Next we examine the major sources of secondary data, including the census, special surveys, simple observation, the Internet, and archival data. Finally, we present content analysis as a method for systematically analyzing data obtained from archival records, documents, and newspapers.

CHAPTER OBJECTIVES

After studying this chapter, you should be able to:

1.   cite the advantages and disadvantages of secondary data analysis in comparison to primary data procedures.

2.   identify the basic elements of the census and the most common statistical units used therein and discuss the "complete count" census.

3.   be familiar with the different sources of secondary data.

4.   be familiar with the role of the Internet in expanding accessibility to sources of information.

5.   describe the various unobtrusive measures: simple observation, public records, and private records.

6.   discuss the major methodological issues in content analysis.

MAIN POINTS

Introduction

The data collection methods discussed so far in the text generate primary data. Increasingly, social scientists make use of data that were previously collected by other investigators, usually for purposes different from the original research objectives; secondary data analysis refers to research findings based on data collected by others.

Why Secondary Data Analysis?

Secondary analysis has a rich intellectual tradition in the social sciences. There are three major kinds of reasons for the increased utilization of secondary data: 1) conceptual-substantive (secondary data may be the only source of data available to study certain research problems), 2) methodological (there are at least five methodological advantages to secondary analysis: it provides opportunities for replication; the availability of data over time makes possible the employment of longitudinal research designs; it may improve measurement; sample size, representativeness, and the number of observations may be increased; and it can be used for triangulation purposes, thus perhaps increasing the credibility of research findings obtained with primary data), and 3) economy.

Limitations of Secondary Data Analysis

Like other data collection methods, secondary analysis has certain limitations. Perhaps the most serious problem is that often it only approximates the kind of data that the investigator would like to have for testing hypotheses. A second problem is that access to such data is difficult. Third, there may be insufficient information about the collection of the data to determine potential sources of bias, errors, or problems with internal or external validity.

The Census

A census is defined as the recording of demographic data of a population in a strictly defined territory, made by the government at a specific time and at regular intervals. The U.S. census of population and housing taken every ten years is called a complete count census and reaches (in theory) every household in the country. Census data are usually provided for two types of geographical clusters: 1) political units such as states, counties, or congressional districts and 2) statistical areas, which are groupings defined for statistical use. There are two major types of error in census data: 1) errors in coverage and 2) errors in content. Census data are provided in two basic formats: 1) printed reports and 2) computer tapes, with the former being the primary source of data.

Searching for Secondary Data

Guidelines for data search include specification of needs, initial familiarization, initial contacts, secondary contacts, accessibility, and analysis and supplemental analyses. The major resources available to would-be secondary analysts searching for data are catalogs, guides, and directories of archives and organizations established to assist researchers.

The Internet

By the end of the 1990s, the "Internet Revolution" had penetrated many aspects of contemporary life. The Internet has contributed to the process of research by expanding accessibility to sources of information. Computers and their peripherals have replaced much of the equipment used to do research. The Internet is a "web" of computers linked together by means of telephone lines. It is a public system that is available to all, free of charge, with the exception of connection charges for on-line services. There is ongoing controversy regarding the regulation of the Internet, and these issues present many challenges to social scientists.

Unobtrusive Measures

An unobtrusive measure is any method of data collection that directly removes the researcher from the set of interactions, events, or behaviors being investigated. These measures range from private and public archives to simple behavior observations of people at work or play, and from physical trace analysis to contrived observations.

Physical trace measures are used to examine physical evidence of some phenomenon. These measures include erosion measures (an activity has worn down a physical object) and accretion measures (physical deposits provide evidence of an activity). Simple observations are the second basic variety of unobtrusive measure. There are four types: observation of exterior body and physical signs, analysis of expressive movement, physical location analysis, and observation of language behavior. Simple observation can be problematic in that observations may be limited to a peculiar population, human observers may make errors, only certain (mainly public) phenomena are available for observation, and simple observational data usually provide only descriptions and not explanations.

Archival Records

Another form of unobtrusive, secondary data is archival records, which constitute a rich source of information that may be studied without direct contact with the entities being observed. There are two major sources of archival information: public records and private records. Four basic kinds of public records can be distinguished: actuarial records, political and judicial records, governmental documents, and the mass media. Unlike public records, private records are difficult to obtain; they include autobiographies, diaries, letters, and essays. A major problem with the use of private documents lies in the need to ensure their authenticity.

Content Analysis

Content analysis is both a means of gathering data and a method of analysis. Instead of observing people's behavior directly or asking them about it, the researcher takes the communications that people have produced and "asks questions" of the communications. Content analysis involves the systematic examination of the content of communications in order to make inferences about the characteristics of the text, antecedents of the message, or effects of the communication.

The content analysis procedure involves the interaction of two processes: specification of the content characteristics to be measured, and application of the rules for identifying and recording the characteristics when they appear in the texts to be analyzed. Five major recording units have been used frequently in content analysis research: words or terms, themes, characters, paragraphs, and items. Content analysis typically involves one of four systems of enumeration: 1) time or space measures examine the amount of time or space devoted to an issue; 2) appearance measures assess whether or not a word or theme appears in a commentary; 3) frequency counts assess how often a theme, word, or character appears in a communication; and 4) intensity measures focus on the degree to which a theme or idea is expressed.

KEY TERMS (page reference in parenthesis)
To assist you in familiarizing yourself with the Key Terms, imagine a series of "short answer" questions that ask you to define each term in your own words, using the text's discussion as a guide.

accretion measures (288)
actuarial records (290)
analysis of expressive
    movements (289)

archival records (290)
authenticity (293)
census block (282)

Census Designated
    Places (282)
census tract (282)

complete count census (281)
content analysis (296)
context unit (298)
erosion measures (288)

language behavior (289)
Metropolitan Statistical Area (MSA) (282)
physical location analysis (289)

recording unit (298)
simple observation (288)
unobtrusive measures (287)

SELF-EVALUATION EXERCISES

Introduction

1. Data collected by previous researchers and used for purposes different from the original reasons for collecting the data are known as _____.

Why Secondary Data Analysis?

2. What are three reasons for the increased use of secondary data analysis?
   1. _____
   2. _____
   3. _____

Limitations of Secondary Data Analysis

3. Identify the major limitations of secondary data.
   1. _____
   2. _____
   3. _____

The Census

4. A census is defined as _____
   _____
   _____
   _____.

5. What are the advantages and disadvantages of complete count and sample count censuses?
   _____
   _____

_____
_____

6.   A census unit which is defined as one or more counties, including a large population nucleus and nearby communities, that have a high degree of interaction is a _____.

7.   _____ are small, locally defined statistical areas with an average population of 4,000.

8.   The U.S. Census of Population and Housing is taken every _____ years.

Searching for Secondary Data

9.   List the six steps in William Trochim's set of guidelines for searching for secondary data.

    1.   _____
    2.   _____
    3.   _____
    4.   _____
    5.   _____
    6.   _____

The Internet

10.   America On-Line and Microsoft Network are both examples of _____ services.

11.   Because the Internet is an international system, it is difficult to _____.

Unobtrusive Measures

12.   What is an unobtrusive measure?

    _____
    _____
    _____

13.   Observing the amount of carpet wear in front of paintings in an art museum to measure the popularity of the paintings would be using what kind of unobtrusive measure? _____

14.   What kind of unobtrusive measure would you be using if you observed the amount of scratch paper students left in trash cans after a mathematics exam to measure the difficulty of the exam? _____

15.   What are the four varieties of simple observation that involve unobtrusive measurement?

    1.   _____

2. _____

3. _____

4. _____

16. Observing how a professor gestures with his or her hands during a lecture would involve the analysis of _____.

Archival Records

17. Suppose you are doing a study of death rates over the last 10 years in communities containing chemical or toxic-waste dumps. To obtain information on death rates, you would need to consult _____.

18. Identify two archival data sources one might consult for a study of presidential voting trends in the last four elections.

    1. _____

    2. _____

19. Identify three kinds of private records.

    1. _____

    2. _____

    3. _____

20. Private records may be inauthentic due to _____ or

    _____.

Content Analysis

21. Content analysis is a method of _____ and a method of

    _____.

22. In what sense is content analysis unobtrusive?

    _____

    _____

23. Identify eight kinds of communications to which the use of content analysis could be applied.

    1. _____

    2. _____

    3. _____

    4. _____

    5. _____

    6. _____

    7. _____

    8. _____

24. The five major recording units used in content analysis are:

1. _____

2. _____

3. _____

4. _____

5. _____

REVIEW TESTS

Multiple-Choice   Place the letter corresponding to the one BEST answer in the space provided.

_____ 1. Which of the following statements about secondary data analysis is NOT true?

    a. Studies based upon secondary data are generally less costly than those using primary data.

    b. Secondary data facilitates the study of phenomena occurring over time.

    c. Studies using secondary data usually have smaller samples than studies using primary data.

    d. Studies using secondary data provide opportunities for replicating previous studies.

_____ 2. An example of a statistical area is a:

    a. Metropolitan Statistical Area (MSA)

    b. precinct

    c. Standard Statistical Unit (SSU)

    d. county

_____ 3. Census tracts are small, locally defined statistical areas with an average population of:

    a. 15,000–25,000

    b. 10,000–15,000

    c. 4,000

    d. more than 25,000

_____ 4.   Which of the following would most likely display census undercount?
- a.   a community in which a large number of persons report higher incomes than they actually have
- b.   a community in which there is a large number of illegal aliens
- c.   a community in which a large number of residents are not registered to vote
- d.   a community in which a large number of residents work on farms

_____ 5.   Which of the following publications would be BEST suited to providing census statistics on unemployment trends?
- a.   *Consumer Expenditure Survey*
- b.   *Annual Housing Survey*
- c.   *America Votes*
- d.   *Current Population Survey*

_____ 6.   An unobtrusive measure is one which:
- a.   uses field experimentation as the main method of data collection
- b.   is often used in survey research
- c.   removes the researcher from events and behavior under study
- d.   relies on laboratory experimentation

_____ 7.   If you were to study changes in birth rates over time in American states, you would be using:
- a.   actuarial records
- b.   accretion measures
- c.   content analysis
- d.   political and judicial records

_____ 8.   Which of the following illustrates the use of accretion measures?

a.   measuring the amount of wear on pencil leads to see how much students wrote on an examination

b.   measuring the underlining in textbooks to see how students study for an examination

c.   measuring footpaths on a college campus to study pedestrian traffic patterns

d.   measuring the scratches on phonograph records to determine the popularity of certain songs

_____ 9.   Which of the following could NOT be subjected to content analysis?

a.   presidential news conferences

b.   televised presidential debates

c.   Karl Marx's _Communist Manifesto_

d.   a Mozart piano concerto

_____ 10.   Which of the following situations would be appropriate for using content analysis?

a.   studying the facial expressions of members of a jury whenever the name of the defendant is mentioned

b.   studying the relationship between legislators' political party affiliation and their legislative votes

c.   studying the relationship between economic conditions and suicide rates in major cities

d.   studying the speeches of presidents to see how often they refer to the issue of inflation

_____ 11.   Probably the most serious disadvantage in using secondary data is that they:

a.   rarely provide the scope and depth that primary data provide

b.   give only an approximation of primary data

c.   offer little opportunity for replication

d.   are more costly than primary data

_____ 12.   If one wanted to measure the extent of the U.S. inflation rate and its
impact on the cost of living, one would find which of the following
sources most valuable?
  a.   *Consumer Expenditure Survey*
  b.   *American Housing Survey*
  c.   *Census User's Guide*
  d.   *Government Guide to the GNP*

_____ 13.   Each of the following is an important public source of archival data
EXCEPT:

  a.   actuarial records, such as birth records
  b.   political and judicial records, such as the *Congressional
       Quarterly Almanac*
  c.   authors' interpretations, such as edited autobiographies
  d.   government documents, such as city budgets

_____ 14.   The content analysis procedure involves the interaction of two processes:
specifying the content characteristics to be analyzed and:
  a.   establishing rules for dealing with the characteristics when
       they appear in the material being analyzed
  b.   analyzing situations in which the observer has no control
       over the behavior in question
  c.   examining physical traces, erosion measures, and accretion
       measures for data that exhibit these characteristics
  d.   determining what sources of data are most appropriate for
       locating the characteristics

_____ 15.   The difference between a recording unit and a context unit in the content
analysis procedure is that a context unit:
  a.   is the smallest body of content in which the appearance of a
       reference is counted
  b.   is used in characterizing a recording unit
  c.   may be a word or character but not a complete sentence of
       paragraph
  d.   must be at least a complete sentence and no smaller unit

True-False   Circle T if the answer is true, F if it is false.

T   F   1.   Studies using secondary data are less expensive and time-consuming than studies using primary data.

T   F   2.   A complete count census is more economical and faster to complete than a census sample.

T   F   3.   CDPs are densely settled population areas without legally defined corporate limits.

T   F   4.   The U.S. Census of Population is taken before and after every presidential election.

T   F   5.   Divorce rates are obtained through actuarial records.

T   F   6.   Accretion measures refer to the wear on physical objects as a result of some behavior.

T   F   7.   Observing the amount of perspiration on a person's forehead to measure amount of stress is an example of expressive movement.

T   F   8.   The type of diary that provides the most personal and authentic account of a person's perceptions and activities over a long period of time is the log.

T   F   9.   The smallest recording unit in content analysis is the sentence.

T   F   10.   Content analysis is a method of data analysis as well as a method of observation.

EXERCISES AND PROJECTS

Project 13-1

After consulting with the reference librarian or government document section of your college library, identify sources of data you could use for research on the following topics.

a.   The legislative votes of congressmen on environmental issues

Source of data:

b.   The numbers of black, white, and Hispanic students attending public school in school districts in your state

Source of data:

c.   The percentage of households in your state that lack sound plumbing facilities

Source of data:

d.   The gross national products (GNPs) of European nations

Source of data:

e.   The number of armed robberies per thousand population in counties of your state

Source of data:

f.   The average acreage of farms in counties of your state

Source of data:

Exercise 13-2

The Internet is of extreme interest to social scientists because of the controversies surrounding it, as well as the web's utility in the actual conduct of research. Do you believe that the Internet should be *regulated*? For example, how do you feel about pornography on the Internet? If you are in favor of regulation, how would you go about implementing such a plan? Write a proposal concerning your strategy in regulating the Internet. If you feel there should be no regulation, ask yourself this question: What if an organization like the Ku Klux Klan were to attempt to dominate various sites on the Internet? Would this change your mind about regulation?

Project 13-3

Assume that you are doing a content analysis of themes of "sex appeal" in television commercials. Specifically, the focus of your research is to show how product advertising attempts to persuade viewing audiences that the use of certain products will improve one's appeal to the opposite sex.

View television advertisements for three commercial products. As you view these advertisements, record appropriate examples of words, themes, visual images, and voice characteristics which you feel communicate messages concerning sex appeal.

Product 1: _____

      Words:

      Themes:

      Visual images:

      Voice characteristics:

Product 2: _____

      Words:

      Themes:

      Visual images:

      Voice characteristics:

Product 3: _____

      Words:

      Themes:

      Visual images:

      Voice characteristics:

CHAPTER 14

DATA PREPARATION AND ANALYSIS

CHAPTER ABSTRACT

In this chapter, we examine common methods of preparing and coding data. We discuss deductive coding--in which researchers derive codes from theory--as well as inductive coding--in which researchers identify categories from data--and provide rules for coding and codebook construction. We address the issue of coding reliability and discuss methods that researchers can use to increase reliability. Finally, we describe various coding devices and the use of computers in storing, processing, accessing, and analyzing data sets.

CHAPTER OBJECTIVES

After studying this chapter, you should be able to:

1. identify the main criteria for coding schemes and the rules of coding, especially the differences between deductive and inductive coding.

2. construct a simple codebook.

3. explain the principle of coding reliability and list the steps involved in its determination.

4. name the different types of coding devices.

5. describe the procedures for editing and cleaning the data.

6. discuss the use of computers in social science research, including the various types of computers and linkages through communication networks.

MAIN POINTS

Coding Schemes

The number assigned to an observation is called a code. Systems of categories used to classify responses or acts are referred to as coding schemes. The main purpose of coding is to simplify the handling of many individual responses by classifying them into a smaller number of groups, each including responses that are similar in content.

Rules of Coding

The initial rule of coding is that the numbers assigned must make intuitive sense. Once intuitive sense has been satisfied, then linkage to theory, mutual exclusivity, exhaustiveness, and detail must be factored into coding decisions. Linkage to theory assumes that the researcher has some idea, from the literature, of what types of responses to expect from a respondent. Theory can be used to construct response categories before the instrument is administered. Thus, deductive coding can be used; the respondents or those who administer the instrument can classify their responses in preestablished categories, as is the case with closed-ended questions. When a study is exploratory or when there is little theory informing the researcher about which responses to expect, inductive coding may be appropriate.

Codebook Construction

Once a coding scheme has been developed for each of the variables used in a research project, this information should be compiled in a codebook. Once the codebook is constructed, the data need to be coded or transferred into a form in which these data will be stored and analyzed. Studies with a well-constructed codebook experience fewer problems involving reliability. Coding reliability is increased by keeping coding schemes simple and by training coders thoroughly. Coding devices include transfer sheets, edge coding, optical scanning, and direct data entry. There are two forms of direct data coding: coding from a questionnaire and coding by telephone interviewing. Computer-assisted telephone interviewing (CATI) is a highly sophisticated system that greatly reduces miscoding. Editing and cleaning the data are important steps in data processing that should always precede analysis of the collected information. Data editing occurs both during and after the coding phase. Data cleaning is the proofreading of the data to catch and correct errors and inconsistent codes.

Using Computers in Social Science Research

Computers are simply tools that allow more ease in storing, processing, accessing, and analyzing data sets. There are currently three basic kinds of computers used to analyze social science data. Mainframe computers are large central-site computers that simultaneously handle the computing needs of many users. Users tend to "time-share" the capacity of the central processing unit so that the greatest number of users can access the computer at any given time. Minicomputers are similar to mainframes in that they can support software packages, which are in turn accessed by multiple users. The number of users is smaller than is typical of mainframes. Dedicated terminals and networked personal computers (PCs) (the third type) access the programs and data files in a miniature version of the time-share model. The major difference between the PC and the other computers is that the PC is self-contained.

KEY TERMS (page reference in parenthesis)
To assist you in familiarizing yourself with the Key Terms, imagine a series of "short answer" questions that ask you to define each term in your own words, using the text's discussion as a guide.

code (304)	data editing (314)	edge coding (312)
codebook (309)	deductive coding (307)	exhaustiveness (306)
coding schemes (305)	detail (307)	inductive coding (307)
data cleaning (314)	direct data entry (312)	mutual exclusivity (306)

SELF-EVALUATION EXERCISES

Coding Schemes

1. The number assigned to an observation is called a _____.
2. The main purpose of coding is to _____
   _____.
3. A deductive coding system is one in which _____
   _____.
4. An inductive coding system in one in which _____
   _____
   _____.
5. If a coding system does not have enough categories for every possible observation to be coded, it is not _____.

6.   If two or more categories of a coding system overlap in such a way that it is not possible for some observations to receive more than one code, the coding system is not _____.

Codebook Construction

7.   What is a codebook?

    _____

    _____

    _____

8.   Once the codebook is constructed, the data need to be _____, or transferred to a form from which someone can enter them into a computer for storage and _____.

9.   The coding of _____ questions generally requires more judgment in classifying responses than the coding of _____ questions.

10.   Name two sources of errors that occur during the coding phase of data analysis.

    1.   _____

    2.   _____

11.   The _____ (less/more) structured an item in a questionnaire, the larger the discrepancy between the respondent's interpretation and that of the coder.

12.   List and define four types of devices used to code raw data.

    1.   _____

    2.   _____

    3.   _____

    4.   _____

13.   The transfer of data into the computer by means of transfer sheets takes place in two stages: _____ and _____. Verification of both steps enhances coding _____.

14.   The most reliable method for coding raw data from a questionnaire is _____. The most sophisticated device that relies on this method is _____.

15.   Proofreading coded data to catch and correct errors and inconsistent codes is known as _____. In large-scale projects, this procedure is typically carried out by _____.

Using Computers in Social Science Research

16.   What are the two basic kinds of computers used to analyze social science data?

    1.   _____

    2.   _____

17. The largest and most powerful of the computers used to analyze social science data are known as _____ computers. Many users can access data in these computers simultaneously through the process known as_____

_____.

18. A statistical package that allows a computer to analyze social science data is referred to by the general term of computer _____.

19. The smallest and simplest type of computer used to analyze social science data is the _____.

REVIEW TESTS

Multiple-Choice Place the letter corresponding to the one BEST answer in the space provided.

_____ 1. Which of the following statements about differences between inductive and deductive coding schemes is true?
   a. As a general rule, deductive coding schemes are more appropriate for coding responses to open-ended questions.
   b. As a general rule, deductive coding schemes are linked to a theory and inductive coding schemes are not.
   c. As a general rule, deductive coding schemes are less rigid than inductive coding schemes.
   d. Exhaustiveness is more important in inductive than in deductive coding schemes.

_____ 2. An inductive coding scheme would most likely be called for in which of the following situations?
   a. posing 30 questions to respondents and asking them to answer "strongly agree", "agree", "disagree", or "strongly disagree"
   b. asking respondents to indicate about how often they have attended religious services in the past year; never, once or twice, more than twice but less than 5 times, more than 5 times
   c. asking respondents why they chose their particular careers
   d. asking respondents to rate various public figures on a scale from 0 to 100, with 0 registering strong disapproval and 100 strong approval

_____ 3.   A coding system that classifies employed persons as "government employee,""self-employed," or "employed in the private sector" violates the criterion that coding systems should be:
   a.   exhaustive
   b.   mutually exclusive
   c.   linked to theory
   d.   detailed

_____ 4.   A coding system that classifies cities as Northeast, Midwest, South, West, and Alabama violates the criterion that coding systems should be:
   a.   exhaustive
   b.   mutually exclusive
   c.   linked to theory
   d.   detailed

_____ 5.   A classification of race/ethnicity into categories of "white" or "black" violates the criterion that coding systems should be:
   a.   exhaustive
   b.   mutually exclusive
   c.   linked to theory
   d.   detailed

_____ 6.   Research indicates that coding reliability is lowest when:
   a.   closed-ended questions are used
   b.   relatively nonstructured material is used
   c.   a codebook is used
   d.   precoded questions are used

_____ 7.   One major source of errors that occur during the coding of raw data from a questionnaire is when:
   a.   modems are used as a means of transmitting data
   b.   data at both the coding and keying steps are verified
   c.   codebooks are precoded and closed-ended questions are used
   d.   respondent and coder interpret a response differently

_____ 8.   If one is looking for the most reliable means of coding raw data from a questionnaire, one would probably choose:
   a.   edge coding
   b.   optical scanning
   c.   computer-assisted telephone interviewing (CATI)
   d.   matched transfer sheets

_____ 9.   "Time-sharing" of a computer's central processing unit is most likely to be possible with what type of computer?
   a.   a mainframe computer
   b.   a minicomputer
   c.   a microcomputer
   d.   a personal computer

_____ 10.   Researchers use two basic kinds of computers to analyze social science data:
   a.   mainframes and minicomputers
   b.   supercomputers and mainframes
   c.   mainframes and personal computers
   d.   personal computers and laptops

True-False   Circle T if the answer is true, F if it is false.

T   F   1.   Most coding schemes for closed-ended items use the deductive approach.

T   F   2.   Coding schemes using the deductive approach are usually formulated prior to collecting data.

T   F   3.   If you were to ask people to explain in their own words what they think is the most important problem facing the country today, most likely you would use the inductive approach for coding responses.

T   F   4.   Inductive coding schemes are generally more flexible than deductive coding schemes.

T   F   5.   Inductive and deductive coding schemes employ different criteria.

T   F   6.   In general, it is better to set up too many than too few categories.

T   F   7.   Transfer sheets and optical scanners are two software packages used to analyze research data.

T   F   8.   The direct entry of data through phone interviews ensures the greatest degree of coding reliability.

T   F   9.   The use of computers in social science research began in the early 1980s.

T   F   10.   The rationale for the use of computers in research has changed drastically over time.

EXERCISES AND PROJECTS

Exercise 14-1

Construct a codebook for the following survey questionnaire. Assume that 100 persons responded to the survey. Your codebook should include (1) the coding scheme for each item and (2) the numerical values assigned to each response

ATTITUDES TOWARD GOVERNMENT SPENDING: A SURVEY

"Hello. My name is _____. Could I ask you a few questions for a project I am doing in my research methods class at _____ College/University?
First, I am going to ask you some questions about how much money you think the government in Washington should spend for several programs and purposes. As I read these items, please tell me whether you think the government in Washington should spend more, spend about the same as now, or spend less.

	Spend More	Spend Same	Spend Less	Undecided
1.	Improving public schools			
2.	Fighting drug abuse			
3.	Reducing pollution			
4.	Improving health care			

	Spend More	Spend Same	Spend Less	Undecided

5.   Solving the problems of big cities
6.   Improving conditions for blacks and other minorities
7.   About how interested would you say you are in what goes on in government and politics?
( ) very interested
( ) somewhat interested
( ) not very interested
( ) not at all interested
8.   On most political issues would you describe yourself as
( ) very liberal
( ) slightly liberal
( ) middle of the road
( ) slightly conservative
( ) very conservative
9.   Generally speaking, do you consider yourself to be a/an
( ) Democrat
( ) Republican
( ) Independent
( ) Other
10.   In your own words, could you please tell me what you think you think is the most important problem facing the country today? (Summarize respondent's answer in spaces below.)

_____

_____

_____

11.   Do you own your home or do you rent? ( ) own ( ) rent
12.   How old are you? _____
13.   Sex of respondent: ( ) Male ( ) Female

That's the end of the interview. Thank you for your time and help."

CHAPTER 15

THE UNIVARIATE DISTRIBUTION

CHAPTER ABSTRACT

In this chapter, we explain the main characteristics of single-variable distributions. First we define and describe frequency distributions, which researchers use to organize their data for statistical analysis. Then, we focus on measures of central tendency and measures of dispersion, which can be used to describe distributions. Finally, we deal with the general form of distributions, emphasizing the normal curve.

CHAPTER OBJECTIVES

After studying this chapter, you should be able to:

1. describe the role of descriptive and inferential statistics in social science research.

2. explain the concept of a frequency distribution and describe its characteristics.

3. be able to use graphs (pie charts, bar charts, and histograms) to describe distributions.

4. calculate the three measures of central tendency: mode, median, and mean.

5. calculate and interpret the measures of dispersion discussed in this chapter: qualitative variation, range, mean deviation, variance, standard deviation, and coefficient of variation.

6. describe the different types of frequency distributions and the concepts related to them.

7. calculate standard scores and employ them in reference to the normal curve.

MAIN POINTS

The Role of Statistics

The field of statistics involves methods for describing and analyzing data and for making decisions or inferences about phenomena represented by the data. Methods in the first category are referred to as descriptive statistics and are used to summarize and organize data in an effective and meaningful way. Methods in the second category are called inferential statistics and are used to make decisions or inferences by interpreting data patterns.

Frequency Distribution

Frequency distributions are used to examine the pattern of response to each of the independent and dependent variables under investigation. A frequency distribution of a single variable, sometimes referred to as a univariate frequency distribution, is the frequency of observations in each category of a variable.

Percentage distributions are a special type of frequency distribution that show what percentage of cases in a distribution occur in each category of a variable.

Using Graphs to Describe Distributions

Graphs provide researchers with an alternative method of displaying the information organized in frequency distributions. Three of the graphs researchers most commonly use are the pie chart, the bar chart, and the histogram; both the pie chart and the bar chart can be used to present data measured at the nominal and ordinal levels; the histogram is used with interval or ratio levels.

Measures of Central Tendency

Measures of central tendency are statistical procedures that reflect a "typical" or an "average" characteristic of a frequency distribution. The three most commonly employed are the mode, the median, and the arithmetic mean.

The mode is the category or the observation that appears most frequently in a distribution.

The median is a positional measure that divides the distribution into two equal parts; it is defined as the observation that is located halfway between the smallest and the largest observations in the distribution.

Percentiles are measures of location, indicating the point below which a given percentage of the values in a distribution fall. The median is a special case of a percentile: the 50th percentile.

The arithmetic mean is the measure of central tendency most frequently used and is defined as the sum total of all observations divided by the number of those observations.

Basic Measures of Dispersion

Measures of central tendency identify the most representative value of the distribution, but a complete description of any distribution requires that the extent of dispersion about this central value be measured. There are various measures of dispersion: qualitative variation, range, mean deviation, variance, standard deviation, and coefficient of variation. The measure of qualitative variation indicates the number of differences among the categories of a distribution and is based upon the number of categories and their respective frequencies.

The range measures the distance between the highest and lowest values of the distribution. The interquartile range is the difference between the lower and upper quartiles; it measures the spread in the middle half of the distribution and is less affected by extreme observations.

Measures of Dispersion Based on the Mean

The simplest way to obtain a measure of deviation is to calculate the average deviation from the arithmetic mean, but the sum of the deviations from the mean is always equal to zero; thus the average deviation will always be zero. To compensate for this property of the mean, each deviation is squared in order to calculate the standard deviation--the measure of dispersion most commonly applied to interval-level data. The standard deviation has various advantages: it is more stable from sample to sample; it has some important mathematical properties that enable the researcher to obtain the standard deviation for two or more groups combined; and its mathematical properties make it a useful measure in more advanced statistical work, especially in the area of statistical inferences.

Computation of the variance and standard deviation is similar to that of the mean deviation, except that instead of taking the deviation's absolute values, we square them, sum the squares, and then divide by the total number of observations. The variance indicates the average squared deviation of values from the mean in a distribution; the standard deviation is the square root of the variance.

The coefficient of variation reflects relative variation; it measures variation in a distribution relative to the mean of the distribution.

Types of Frequency Distributions

Frequency distributions can display different shapes. In symmetrical distributions, the mean will coincide with the median and the mode. In skewed distributions, there will be discrepancies between these measures. In a negatively skewed distribution, the mean will be pulled in the direction of the lower scores; in a positively skewed distribution, the mean will be located closer to the high scores.

One type of symmetrical distribution is the normal curve, wherein a fixed proportion of cases falls between the mean and any given point in the distribution. Standard scores express the distance between a specific observation and the mean in terms of standard deviation units.

KEY TERMS (page reference in parenthesis)
To assist you in familiarizing yourself with the Key Terms, imagine a series of "short answer" questions that ask you to define each term in your own words, using the text's discussion as a guide.

arithmetic mean (331)
bar chart (327)
coefficient of variation (341)
descriptive statistics (321)
frequency distribution (321)
histogram (328)

inferential statistics (321)
interquartile range (337)
measure of qualitative
  variation (335)
median (330)
mode (329)

normal curve (344)
range (337)
skewed distribution (343)
standard deviation (340)
standard score (345)
variance (339)

SELF-EVALUATION EXERCISES

The Role of Statistics

1.   _____ statistics enable a researcher to summarize large quantities of data.

2.   To make decisions based on the interpretation of data patterns, we use _____ statistics.

Frequency Distribution

3.   A display of number of observations in each category of a variable is called a(n) _____.

4.   Construct a frequency distribution of the variable "political affiliation" for a class of 200 students of whom 28 percent are Republicans, 51 percent are Democrats, 18 percent are Independents, and 3 percent have no political affiliation.

Political Affiliation	*f*
_____	_____
_____	_____
_____	_____
_____	_____

5.   One must calculate _____ and _____ in order to compare one frequency distribution to another.

6.   Consider the following frequency distributions, which display hypothetical data on crimes in three cities. How do these cities compare in terms of the incidence of armed robbery?

_____

_____

_____

Podunk

Crime	*f*
Murder	30
Rape	60
Armed Robbery	120
Burglary	90

Townville

Crime	*f*
Murder	100
Rape	75
Armed Robbery	125
Burglary	200

Cityview

Crime	*f*
Murder	35
Rape	105
Armed Robbery	210
Burglary	350

Using Graphs to Describe Distributions

7.   _____ provide researchers with an alternative method of displaying the information organized in frequency distributions.

8.   Both the _____ and the _____ can be used to present data measured at the nominal and ordinal levels.

9.   Researchers use the _____ to display data measured at interval or ratio levels.

10.   Unlike the bar chart, the _____ cannot be used to display information for more than one variable.

Measures of Central Tendency

11.   Choosing a single value to represent a distribution involves the use of a

_____

12.   The three most commonly used measures of central tendency are _____, _____, and _____.

13.   The value or category in a distribution that occurs most frequently is called the _____.

14. The main advantage of the mode is that it _____.
15. The value that divides a distribution into two equal halves is the

    _____.
16. The point in a distribution above which 25 percent of the observations lie is
    the _____.
17. The measure of central tendency that takes into account all values in a
    distribution is the _____.
18. The mean is obtained by _____ the scores and dividing by the

    _____.
19. A disadvantage of the mean is that it is _____.
20. For each of the following, indicate which measure of central tendency--
    mode, median, or mean--would be most appropriate.
    1. The ages of professors at your college or university

       _____
    2. The number and percentage of professors in English, Mathematics,
       Science, and History at your college or university

       _____
    3. The length of employment (0-years, 5–10 years, 10–15 years, 15–20
       years, more than 20 years) of professors at your college or university

       _____
    4. Individual incomes in your home town or city _____
    5. The numbers of freshmen, sophomores, juniors, and seniors in your
       research methods class _____

Basic Measures of Dispersion

21. Measures of dispersion reflect the degree of _____ away from a
    _____ in a distribution.
22. The degree of variation in a nominal distribution is indicated by the _____

    _____.
23. A measure of qualitative variation equal to one indicates _____

    _____.
24. The range is the difference between the _____ value and the
    _____ value in a distribution.
25. The range is a crude measure of dispersion because

    _____

    _____.
26. The interquartile range is a more reliable stable measure of dispersion than
    the range because

    _____.

Measures of Dispersion Based on the Mean

27.   In calculating the average deviation, the sum of the deviations from the
       mean is equal to _____.
28.   The square root of the variance is the _____.
29.   The standard deviation is a measure that expresses dispersion in terms of
       the _____ of measurement.
30.   If one has two distributions that have very different means, the measure of
       dispersion one should use to compare the distribution is the

       _____.

Types of Frequency Distributions

31.   A distribution that can be divided in half so that each half is a mirror image
       of the other is called a _____ distribution.
32.   A distribution with more extreme cases in one direction than the other is
       called a _____ distribution.
33.   When the mode, median, and mean are identical, the distribution is

       _____.
34.   If the mean of a distribution is 28 and the mode is 36, the distribution is
       _____ skewed.
35.   The normal curve is based upon a(n) _____ number of observations.
36.   On a test, a class has an average score of 76 and a standard deviation of 6.
       The proportion of scores between 82 and 88 is _____.
37.   A standard score expresses the distance between an individual observation
       and the _____ in terms of _____ units.
38.   If Sally's score on a test is equal to the class mean, Sally's Z score would be

       _____.

REVIEW TESTS

Multiple-Choice   Place the letter corresponding to the one BEST answer in the
                     space provided.

_____ 1.   The measure of central tendency that takes into account all the values in the distribution is the:
   a.   median
   b.   mean
   c.   percentile
   d.   mode

_____ 2.   Which of the following would be the most desirable measure of central tendency for a distribution of schoolchildren's ages?
   a.   mode
   b.   mean
   c.   standard deviation
   d.   range

_____ 3.   The measure of central tendency known as the median is the:
   a.   most frequently occurring value in a distribution
   b.   halfway point between the smallest and largest observation in a distribution
   c.   arithmetic average of observations
   d.   range between the lowest and highest observations

_____ 4.   Which of the following does NOT characterize a normal distribution?
   a.   It is based upon 100 observations.
   b.   It is symmetrical and bell-shaped.
   c.   The mode, median, and mean are the same.
   d.   A single mathematical formula describes the proportion of observations lying between the mean and various points in the distribution.

_____ 5.   Which of the following measures of dispersion would be appropriate for nominal data?
   a.   mean deviation
   b.   standard deviation
   c.   measure of qualitative variation
   d.   lambda

_____ 6.   A distribution which contains more extreme low scores than extreme high scores would be called:
   a.   symmetrical
   b.   bimodal
   c.   positively skewed
   d.   negatively skewed

_____ 7.   Consider the following distribution: 18, 21, 24, 27, 30. The value 24 is the:
   a.   mode
   b.   median
   c.   mean
   d.   median and mean

_____ 8.   Which measure of central tendency can be used to describe a distribution at any level of measurement—nominal, ordinal or interval?
   a.   mode
   b.   median
   c.   mean
   d.   standard deviation

_____ 9.   Consider the following distribution: 16, 42, 45, 47, 47, 49, 50. Which measure of central tendency would provide the LEAST meaningful description of this distribution?
   a.   mode
   b.   median
   c.   mean
   d.   range

_____ 10.   In a sample, a researcher found 18 Democrats, 27 Republicans, and 9 Independents. What is the measure of qualitative variation for this sample?
   a.   0.81
   b.   54
   c.   791
   d.   972

_____ 11.   The following curves depicting the distribution of grades for three different political science classes.

CLASS 1

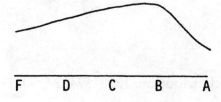

F   D   C   B   A

CLASS 2

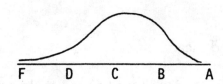

F   D   C   B   A

CLASS 3

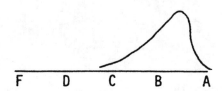

F   D   C   B   A

Which class had the highest standard deviation?
 a. 1
 b. 2
 c. 3
 d. It is impossible to tell on the basis of the information provided.

_____ 12.   A researcher lists the categories of a single variable under investigation and counts the number of observations in each. In so doing, the researcher is constructing a(n):
 a. interquartile range
 b. percentage distribution by response category
 c. univariate frequency distribution
 d. normal distribution curve

_____ 13.   Consider the following list of numbers: 1, 2, 3, 4, 9, 9, 9, 9, 9, 9. Which of the following statements about this list is true?
      a.   The mode and mean are both 6.4.
      b.   The mean and the median are both 6.4.
      c.   The median and mode are both 9.
      d.   The median, mode, and mean are all 9.

_____ 14.   The measure of qualitative variation in nominal distributions is the:
      a.   fixed proportion of observations that lie between the mean and fixed units of standard deviations
      b.   number of observations that fall into each of several categories
      c.   number representing a "typical" or an "average" characteristic of the distribution
      d.   ratio between the total observed differences and the maximum possible differences

_____ 15.   In a distribution with a mean of 100 and a standard deviation of 10, a score of 20 would yield a standard, or Z, of:
      a.   - 5
      b.   +5
      c.   - 8
      d.   +8

True-False   Circle T if the answer is true, F if it is false.

T   F   1.   It is possible to have a distribution that has more than one mode.

T   F   2.   The median splits a frequency distribution into two equal halves.

T   F   3.   If persons were classified as married, single, divorced, or widowed, the appropriate measure of central tendency would be the mean.

T   F   4.   In contrast to the range, the interquartile range is less affected by extreme values.

T   F   5.   Two distributions could have the same median even if they have different means.

T   F   6.   For normal data the appropriate measure of dispersion is the measure of qualitative variation.

T   F   7.   In a skewed distribution the mode, median, and mean are the same.

T   F   8.   In a normal distribution approximately 50 percent of the observations lie within a range of +1 standard deviation.

T   F   9.   Z scores (or standard scores) are individual scores which lie beyond + standard deviations in a normal distribution.

T   F   10.   The coefficient of variation should be used when comparing groups that have substantially different means.

EXERCISES AND PROJECTS

Exercise 15-1

Here is a frequency distribution displaying grouped data on the percentage of voting-age persons registered to vote in 162 counties. Determine the median percentage of voter registration.

Percent Voter Registration	f (counties)
0–9%	2
10–19	6
20–29	4
30–39	16
40–49	26

Percent Voter Registration	f (counties)
50–59	36
60–69	32
70–79	27
80–89	11
90–100	2

Median percentage: _____

The League of Women Voters is planning to conduct voter registration drives in those counties which are in the lowest third in terms of the percent of voting-age persons registered to vote. What is the highest voter-registration percentage a county could have in order to qualify for a registration drive?

_____

Exercise 15-2

Below is a list of 25 U.S. Senators and their hypothetical ratings on a "political ideology" scale ranging from a score of 1 (very liberal) to 10 (very conservative).

Abraham	(7)	Helms	(10)	
Akaka	(6)	Kennedy		(1)
Ashcroft	(7)	Leahy		(4)
Bradley	(3)	Levin		(8)
Byrd	(5)	Lugar		(7)
Campbell	(6)	Mikulski		(7)
D'Amato	(8)	Moynihan		(4)
Daschle	(7)	Nunn		(7)
Dodd	(4)	Pell		(4)
Dole	(7)	Simon		(6)
Garn	(8)	Thurmond		(9)
Harkin	(6)	Wellstone		(5)

Based upon these scores, determine the following:

a.   Mode _____
b.   Mean _____
c.   Standard deviation _____
d.   Standard score (Z) for Senator Dodd _____

e.　　Is this distribution positively or negatively skewed? Explain your answer.

_____

_____

_____

Exercise 15-3

The Democratic Campaign Committee of the U.S. House of Representatives provided financial assistance in 1986 to Democratic candidates seeking election in "competitive" districts. The committee defined a competitive district as one in which the Democratic share of the 1982 vote was between 45 and 55 percent. Research assistants to the committee have found that the Democratic vote in 1982 had a mean of 52 percent and a standard deviation of 8.3. Assuming a normal distribution, determine the percentage of House districts that were "competitive" in 1982 and in which Democratic candidates received financial assistance.

Exercise 15-4

a.　　On the basis of the following set of sample data, calculate an appropriate measure of central tendency to determine whether men or women donated blood more frequently

Men		**Women**	
Number of Donations	f	**Number of Donations**	f
0	23	0	36
1	36	1	27
2	18	2	21
3	14	3	18
4	9	4	2
5	6	5	6
6	2	6	7
	108		117

b.   Using the data above, determine whether there is a greater variability in the amount of blood donation among men or among women.

c.   Using the data above, group the data into intervals 2 units wide. Then calculate the mean, median, and standard deviation for the two samples. Why do you get different values from those calculated in (a) and (b) above?

Exercise 15-5

Which of the following two classes is more racially heterogeneous (has more racial variability)? Base your conclusions on an appropriate measure of dispersion.

Class X

Race	f
Caucasian	21
African American	8
Native American	2
Asian American	3
	34

Class Y

Race	f
Caucasian	16
African American	4
Asian American	4
	24

Calculate the coefficient of variation for the male and female distributions given above.

Exercise 15-6

Using the following set of values, (1) construct a frequency distribution, (2) construct a percentage distribution, (3) determine the interquartile range for the distribution, and (4) determine the median weight for this group. (Use appropriate interval widths.)

Weights of 32 New Members of TOPS (Take Off Pounds Sensibly)

203 142 169 188 128 267 153 122 180 216 194 118 134 202 198 155
176 188 166 233 175 145 133 109 118 157 130 193 124 111 109 126

Project 15-7

Do a brief study of your transportation usage (for a few days). Keep track of how much time you spend on each trip and what type of transportation you take (don't forget walking if you use it to get to anyplace that might be reached by some other method of transportation).

1. Once you have collected sufficient data (on, say 20 or more trips), calculate the mean and median time spent on your trips. Now calculate the variance and standard deviation for these data. (You might find it interesting to compare these statistics with those of your friends or classmates.)

2. Construct a percentage distribution to indicate what percentage of your trips involve each mode of transportation. Determine how much variability there is in your use of transportation.

CHAPTER 16

BIVARIATE ANALYSIS

CHAPTER ABSTRACT

In this chapter, we explore the concept of relationships between two variables and examine different methods for measuring bivariate relationships. In the first section, we discuss the concept of bivariate relationship; the second section describes nominal measures of relationship; the third deals with ordinal measures of relationship; and the last section presents interval measures of relationship.

CHAPTER OBJECTIVES

After studying this chapter, you should be able to:

1.   explain the concept of relationship between two variables.

2.   explain the principle of covariation and construct a bivariate table.

3.   explain the notion of proportional reduction in prediction error as a measure of the relationship between variables.

4.   calculate and interpret the various measures of association that are discussed in the chapter.

5.   identify which measures of association are appropriate for given levels of measurement.

MAIN POINTS

The Concept of Relationship

A basic form of analysis in the social sciences involves the examination of relationships--whether certain categories or values of one variable are more or less likely to occur in common with certain values or categories of a second variable.

The first step in examining a relationship between two variables is the construction of a bivariate table. A bivariate table is one in which two variables have been cross-classified; such tables are used in the examination and presentation of relationships between variables. A generally useful way of summarizing a bivariate table and comparing its univariate distributions to assess relationship is by expressing its frequencies as percentages. Percentaging tables is appropriate whenever the variables are nominal, but the use of percentages is predominant even when the variables being analyzed are ordinal or interval.

Measurement of Relationship

There are various statistical techniques that allow researchers to assess the extent to which two variables are associated by a single summarizing measure. Such measures of relationship, often referred to as correlation coefficients, reflect the strength and direction or association between the variables and the degree to which one variable can be predicted from the other. The notion of prediction is inherent in the concept of covariation. When two variables covary, it is possible to use one to predict the other; when they do not, information about one will not enable the prediction of the other.

The degree to which two variables are related may be assessed in terms of the extent to which knowing values of one variable (the independent variable) allows researchers to increase the accuracy with which the other (dependent) variable can be predicted, compared with predictions made without knowing values of the independent variable. This is known as the principle of proportional reduction of error, and a number of commonly used measures of association are based upon this principle.

Nominal Measures of Relationship

Measures of association must be selected on the basis of the level of measurement reflected in the data under analysis. Lambda, or the Guttman coefficient of predictability, is an asymmetrical coefficient, as it reflects relationships between variables in one direction only.

Lambda has a limitation in situations where the modal frequencies of the independent variable are all concentrated in one category of the dependent variable.

Ordinal Measures of Relationship

Several measures of relationship for ordinal data are based on the concepts of same-order pairs, different-order or inverse-order pairs, and tied pairs.

Gamma is a measure of the preponderance of same-order or different-order pairs among nontied pairs in a bivariate table of ordinal data.

Kendall's tau-*b* takes into account pairs tied on either variable, thereby correcting a deficiency of gamma. However, tau-*b* does not have such a clear-cut interpretation as gamma.

Interval Measures of Relationship

Measures of relationship for interval data are more precise than for lower levels of measurement, because they are based on actual numeric values rather than on membership in categories.

The relationship between two linear variables is frequently examined and expressed by the use of linear regression. The task of regression is to find some algebraic expression by which to represent the functional relationship between the variables. The equation $Y = a + bX$ is a linear regression equation, meaning the function describing the relation between the independent variable (X) and the dependent variable (Y) is a straight line. The regression equation, however, is only a prediction rule; thus, there are discrepancies between actual observations and the ones predicted. The goal is to construct such an equation that the deviations, or error of prediction, will be at a minimum. If a specific criterion is adopted in determining a and b of the linear equation, it is possible to create a function that will minimize the variance around the regression line. This is the criterion of least squares, which minimizes the sum of the squared differences between the observed Y's and the Y's predicted with the regression equation.

Pearson's product moment correlation coefficient (r) provides a single statistic that describes the strength and direction of the relationship between two interval variables. The square of r can be interpreted as the proportional reduction in prediction error afforded by the relationship between two variables. It is therefore comparable to several other measures discussed in this chapter.

KEY TERMS (page reference in parenthesis)
To assist you in familiarizing yourself with the Key Terms, imagine a series of "short answer" questions that ask you to define each term in your own words, using the text's discussion as a guide.

correlation coefficient (361)   Kendall's tau-*b* (373)   proportional reduction
criterion of least   lambda (Guttman   of error (362)
   squares (377)   coefficient of   regression line (375)
error of prediction (377)   predictability) (364)
gamma (370)   Pearson's *r* (380)

SELF-EVALUATION EXERCISES

Introduction

1.   After summarizing the distributional properties of single variables, the next step in data analysis is _____.

The Concept of Relationship

2.   When we say that a relationship exists between two variables, we mean that
_____
_____.

3.   The first step in examining a relationship between two variables is the construction of a(n) _____.

4.   In a bivariate table, the column variable is usually the _____ and the row variable is usually the _____.

5.   A bivariate table is actually a series of _____ distributions.

6.   In a bivariate table, when the categories of one variable are evenly distributed across the categories of the other variable, the two variables are said to be
_____.

7.   When the variables of a bivariate distribution are nominal, the _____ can be used as a measure of covariation.

8.   Examine the following table, and then answer these questions.

Race

	African American	White	Total
Voting Intention			
Yes	150	800	950
No	250	500	750
Total	400	1,300	

1.   What percentage of whites intend to vote? _____
2.   What percentage of African Americans intend to vote? _____
3.   How many people do not intend to vote? _____
4.   How many people are data presented for? _____
5.   Is there an association between race and voting intentions? _____

Measurement of Relationship

9.   Statistical measures of relationship measure the degree to which
      _____.

10.   The principle of proportional reduction of error is used to compare the number
      of inaccurate predictions of a dependent variable made _____
      _____ to the number of inaccurate predictions made _____
      _____.

Nominal Measures of Relationship

11.   Lambda is a(n) _____ statistic whose values range from _____
      to _____.
12.   Lambda is useful for calculating relationships between _____.
13.   A lambda value of .50 would indicate that _____
      _____
      _____.

14.   The value of lambda represents the amount of error reduced by introducing an independent variable to predict the dependent variable compared to guessing the _____ of the dependent variable.

Ordinal Measures of Relationship

15.   When observations display the same ranking on two ordinal variables, the relationship is said to be _____.

16.   If we found that as class standing (freshman, sophomore, junior, senior) increases, satisfaction with college decreases, the relationship would be described as _____.

17.   If we found that freshmen, sophomores, juniors, and seniors are equally satisfied with college, what could we say about the relationship between class standing and satisfaction?

_____

18.   Most ordinal measures of association are based on the _____ concept.

19.   Gamma is a(n) _____ statistic. Its values range from -1.0, indicating _____, to +1.0, indicating _____.

20.   The main weakness of gamma is _____.

21.   If there are many ties in a table, a measure called _____, which incorporates ties rather than excluding them, can be used.

Interval Measures of Relationship

22.   Measures of association based on interval data enable more _____ than measures of association for nominal or ordinal data.

23.   For interval data, a function is linear if values of X and Y can be plotted as _____.

24.   In the regression equation $Y = a + bX$, the letter a represents _____ _____and the letter b represents _____.

25.   Suppose the regression equation $Y = 32.6 + 4X$ expresses the relationship between the Republican percentage of the vote (Y) and the percentage of the work force in white-collar occupations (X) in selected counties. What Republican percentage of the vote would you predict for a county with 62 percent white-collar employment? _____

26.   The best guess for any given value of an interval distribution is the _____.

27.   The graphic device for displaying the bivariate distribution of interval variables is the _____.

28. The standard error of estimate is a measure of _____

     _____ .

29. When there is no correlation between two interval variables, the Pearson
     correlation coefficient, r, is _____ .

30. The square of Pearson's r indicates the _____

     _____ .

31. The magnitude of Pearson's r is determined by _____

     _____ .

REVIEW TESTS

Multiple-Choice   Place the letter corresponding to the one BEST answer in the space
                      provided.

_____ 1. A bivariate table is one in which:
          a. a single variable is broken down into two categories
          b. a dependent variable is cross-classified by two or more
              independent variables
          c. a dependent variable is cross-classified by an independent
              variable
          d. there are two rows and two columns

_____ 2. To say that two variables covary is to say that:
          a. a causal relationship exists
          b. the values of one variable can be used to predict the values
              of the other variable
          c. the variables have nothing in common
          d. the variables are mutually dependent on each other

_____ 3. When two variables are ordinal, the _____ of the univariate distributions
          can be used to measure covariation.
          a. modes
          b. medians
          c. means
          d. standard deviation

_____ 4.   The principle upon which measures of association are based, that knowledge of an independent variable will improve our ability to predict the values of a dependent variable, is known as:
     a.   proportional reduction of error
     b.   sampling validity
     c.   normal distribution
     d.   curvilinearity

_____ 5.   A lambda value of -.50 would indicate:
     a.   a moderately strong relationship between two variables
     b.   a curvilinear relationship
     c.   that the independent variable improves prediction of the dependent variable by 50 percent
     d.   an error in calculation

_____ 6.   A study of voting behavior in the 1988 presidential election finds that of 100 people surveyed, 58 voted for Bush and 42 voted for Dukakis. Suppose it were also found that all 58 Bush voters described themselves as conservative and all 42 Dukakis voters described themselves as liberal. The lambda coefficient for the relationship between the independent variable—ideology (liberal-conservative)—and the dependent variable—vote (Bush-Dukakis)—would be:
     a.   1.0
     b.   -1.0
     c.   0
     d.   100

_____ 7.   The measure of association which determines the degree to which the ranking of a case on one ordinal variable may be predicted if we know its ranking on a second ordinal variable is:
     a.   standard deviation
     b.   lambda
     c.   gamma
     d.   Pearson's _r_

_____ 8.   If two ordinal variables are compared, and it is found that when one ranks high, the other ranks low, the relationship is:
- a.   positive
- b.   inverse
- c.   curvilinear
- d.   skewed

_____ 9.   If we were to encounter a large number of cases that tie on ranks of two ordinal variables, the appropriate measure of association would be:
- a.   lambda
- b.   gamma
- c.   Pearson's r
- d.   Kendall's tau-b or tau-c

_____ 10.   A perfect linear relationship between two interval variables, X and Y, means that:
- a. X and Y are unrelated
- b.   pairs of X and Y values can be plotted as a straight line
- c. X and Y are negatively associated
- d.   when X increases by one unit Y increases by two units.

_____ 11. $Y = a + bX$ is the formula for:
- a.   linear regression
- b.   Pearson's correlation
- c.   lambda coefficient
- d.   standard deviation

_____ 12.   Suppose we have found that the equation $Y = 56 + 7.5X$ represents the relationship between scores of a mathematics exam (Y) and the amount of study time in hours (X). If a student studies four hours, we would predict that his or her exam score will be:
- a.   60
- b.   67.5
- c.   85
- d.   90

_____ 13.   If one were exploring a relationship between years of schooling and income, the most appropriate measure of association would be:
   a.   standard deviation
   b.   lambda
   c.   Kendall's tau-*b*
   d.   Pearson's *r*

_____ 14.   A Pearson's *r* of -1.0 would indicate a(n):
   a.   perfect inverse association
   b.   complete absence of association
   c.   perfect positive association
   d.   error in calculation

_____ 15.   Observe the following scatter diagram.

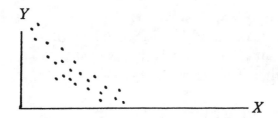

The best way to describe this relationship would be:
   a.   strong positive
   b.   weak positive
   c.   weak inverse
   d.   strong inverse

True-False   Circle T is the answer is true, F is it is false.

T   F   1.   In constructing bivariate tables, it is customary for the categories of the independent variable to be arrayed across the rows.

T   F   2.   The first step in examining the relationship between two nominal or ordinal variables is calculating a correlation coefficient.

T   F   3.   In examining the relationship between age and income, the mode can be used as a measure of covariation.

T   F   4.   Lambda is a symmetrical statistic which varies from +1 to -1.

T   F   5.   Correlation coefficients measure the degree to which one variable can be predicted from another.

T   F   6.   In the proportional reduction of error formula *(b-a)/b*, the term *a* stands for the number of incorrect predictions of a dependent variable before introduction of an independent variable.

T   F   7.   If two ordinal variables are compared, and it is found that the ranks of one variable are evenly distributed across the ranks of the second variable, the relationship is said to be positive.

T   F   8.   Tied pairs are excluded from the computation of gamma.

T   F   9.   A Pearson's *r* of +1.0 indicates a perfect linear relationship between two variables.

T   F   10.   If the equation $Y = 75 + 3X$ represents the relationship between student scores on a test (Y) and the amount of time in hours (X), we can say that it takes 3 hours of study to make a score of 75.

EXERCISES AND PROJECTS

Exercise 16-1

Using the following data for 30 survey respondents, construct a bivariate table displaying the relationship between age and whether people voted in the 1988 election. Arrange the independent variable, age, in three categories: young (18–34), middle-aged (35–54), old (55 and older). Make sure your table follows the guidelines for bivariate table construction outlined in the text.

Age	Voted in 1988?	Age	Voted in 1988?
42	yes	41	yes

Age	Voted in 1988?	Age	Voted in 1988?
36	no	35	no
53	yes	18	no
19	no	75	yes
72	no	44	yes
57	yes	39	no
40	yes	20	no
22	yes	68	yes
21	no	25	yes
65	no	30	no
50	yes	48	yes
20	yes	59	no
81	yes	72	no
30	yes	21	no
38	no	46	yes

Exercise 16-2

You have surveyed 200 respondents to test the hypothesis that political ideology (liberal, moderate, conservative) is related to the region of the country (Northeast, Midwest, South) in which people live. Treating region as the independent variable and political ideology as the dependent variable, determine the lambda coefficient for the following data.

Ideology   **Region**

	Northeast	Midwest	South
Liberal	40	16	8
Moderate	20	34	20
Conservative	14	16	32

Exercise 16-3

In a random survey, 124 lower-class, middle-class, and upper-class respondents were asked: "How important is having a college education to getting ahead in life? Do you think it is very important, somewhat important, or not very important?" The hypothetical results of the survey follow. Calculate the gamma coefficient. What does the value of gamma tell you about the relationship between social-class standing and attitudes toward college education?

Importance of College	Social Class		
	Lower	Middle	Upper
Not important	13	12	6
Somewhat important	9	14	10
Very important	8	28	24

Exercise 16.4

The following hypothetical data show the daily alcohol consumption (in ounces) and the yearly job absenteeism rate (in days) of 12 workers. Determine the regression equation for predicting the number of workdays missed for an employee who consumes 12 ounces of alcohol daily.

Daily Alcohol Consumption (in ounces)	Job Absenteeism (in days)
0	2
1	3
1	3
2	2
2	3
3	4
4	5
4	6
5	5
6	6
6	7
7	5

CHAPTER 17

CONTROL, ELABORATION, AND

MULTIVARIATE ANALYSIS

CHAPTER ABSTRACT

This chapter focuses on the methods that researchers use to analyze more than two variables. The analysis of more than two variables serves three major functions in empirical research: control, elaboration, and prediction. The first function substitutes for the mechanism of experimental control when it is lacking; the second clarifies bivariate relationships by introducing intervening or conditional variables; the third function is served by analyzing two or more independent variables to account for the variation in the dependent variable. This chapter discusses ways in which a third variable may enter into empirical research. First, we consider the strategy of controlling for a third variable through elaboration. Then, we examine multivariate counterparts to the bivariate measures of relations. Finally, we examine the techniques of causal modeling and path analysis.

CHAPTER OBJECTIVES

After studying this chapter, you should be able to:

1. explain the concepts of control and elaboration.

2. describe cross-tabulation and partial correlation as methods of control, and use these techniques in determining whether relationships are spurious.

3. describe multiple regression as a control operation and interpret a multiple regression equation.

4. explain the technique of multivariate analysis.

5. define causal models, discuss the techniques of path analysis, and estimate path coefficients.

MAIN POINTS

Control

Although two variables may be associated, they are not necessarily causally related. By using methods that control other factors, researchers are able to obtain evidence about whether an independent variable has a causal influence on a dependent variable.

In quasi-experimental designs, statistical techniques substitute for the experimental method of control. These techniques are employed during data analysis rather than at the data collection stage. There are three methods of statistical control: cross-tabulation, partial correlation, and multiple regression.

Methods of Control

Cross-tabulation involves the division of the sample into subgroups according to the categories of the controlled variable; thus, a form of control is exerted that provides evidence about the causal influence of the independent variable on the dependent variable.

A partial table shows the extent of relationship between two variables within a single category of some third variable. If an original relationship disappears in partial tables based on an antecedent third variable, the relationship is spurious and not meaningful. If the original relationship changes in the partial tables, but does not completely disappear, the relationship is nonspurious and should be examined further to determine the conditions that bring about the relationship. If the original relationship remains in the partial tables, the third variable does not account for the original relationship.

Elaboration

Elaboration analysis involves considering the nature of the effect of a third variable on a bivariate relationship. If the third variable intervenes between the independent and dependent variables, and the original relationship changes under conditions of the third variable, the third variable clarifies how the variables are related. If the third variable precedes both the independent and the dependent variable, and the original relationship changes under conditions of the third variable, the result specifies the condition under which the relationship exists.

Partial correlation is a statistical method for controlling the effects of a third variable on a bivariate relationship. The partial correlation coefficient measures the extent to which two interval variables are related. This method can be extended to simultaneously remove the effects of several variables if they have been measured and are interval-level variables.

Multiple regression is a simple extension of bivariate regression allowing for an assessment of the relationship between two variables while controlling for the effect of others.

Multivariate Analysis: Multiple Relationships

Because there are usually several determinants for any dependent variable, social scientists often use a method called multiple regression analysis to specify how a set of independent variables in combination influence a dependent variable. To examine the combined effect of all the independent variables, the coefficient of determination, r-squared is computed. The square root of r-squared indicates the correlation between all independent variables taken together with the dependent variable; it is thus denoted as the coefficient of multiple correlation.

Causal Models and Path Analysis

A technique known as causal modeling has been developed to combine theoretical knowledge of relationships between variables with empirical evidence about these relationships and hence to provide evidence about causal relationships within a set of variables.

Path analysis is a technique that uses both bivariate and multiple linear regression equations to test the causal relations among the variables in the model. This procedure involves three major steps: 1) the drawing of a path diagram based on a theory or a set of hypotheses, 2) the calculation of path coefficients using regression techniques, and 3) the determination of indirect effects.

KEY TERMS (page reference in parenthesis)
To assist you in familiarizing yourself with the Key Terms, imagine a series of "short answer" questions that ask you to define each term in your own words, using the text's discussion as a guide.

conditional variable (395)   interaction (395)   partial tables (391)
control variable (388)   intervening variable (394)   path analysis (406)
cross-tabulation (387)   multiple regression (400)   path coefficient (406)
elaboration (394)   partial correlation (399)   spurious relation (387)
indirect effect (407)

SELF-EVALUATION EXERCISES

Introduction

1.   What three purposes are served by analyzing more than two variables?
     1.   _____
     2.   _____
     3.   _____

Control

2.   A relationship between two variables that is due to some third or extraneous variable is said to be _____.
3.   Explain the general concept and process of control.

     _____
     _____
     _____
     _____

4.   The three major methods of statistical control are _____, _____, and _____.
5.   How do experimental and quasi-experimental research designs differ with respect to methods of control?

     _____
     _____
     _____
     _____

Methods of Control

6.   As a method of control in quasi-experimental research, _____ is comparable to _____ in experimental research.

7.   The bivariate tables that result from doing a cross-tabulation within each condition of the control variable are called _____ tables.

8.   Explain the four steps involved in the cross-tabulation method of control.

     1.   _____
     2.   _____
     3.   _____
     4.   _____

9.   In cross-tabulation, what would have to occur in order to determine that a bivariate relationship is spurious?

     _____
     _____
     _____

10. What is the major limitation of cross-tabulation?

     _____
     _____
     _____

Elaboration

11. How does elaboration differ from control in multivariate analysis?

     _____
     _____
     _____

12. What is the difference between an intervening variable and a conditional variable?

     _____
     _____
     _____

13. Interaction involves _____.

14. Interaction can be inferred whenever the relative size or direction of the original bivariate relationship is more pronounced in one category of the _____ than in another.

15. Name the three classes of conditions suggested by Hyman for most bivariate associations used in the analysis of interactions.

     1.   _____

2. _____

3. _____

16. A partial correlation coefficient tells us _____.
    _____

17. A partial correlation involving one control variable is known as a
    _____.

18. The symbol for the partial correlation between variables X and Z with variable Y
    controlled would be _____.

19. Explain the terms of the multiple regression equation:
    $$Y = a + b_1x_1 + b_2x_2$$

    Y _____

    a _____

    b_1x_1 _____

    b_2x_2 _____

20. A multiple-regression equation describes the _____ relationship
    between independent and dependent variables.

21. In multiple regression, the standardized b coefficients are known as
    _____.

22. The multiple regression coefficient measures _____
    _____
    _____

Multivariate Analysis: Multiple Relationships

23. The coefficient of determination tells us _____
    _____
    _____
    _____

Causal Models and Path Analysis

24. What two kinds of evidence are necessary to infer a causal relationship between
    two variables?
    1. _____
    2. _____

25. What are the two simplifying assumptions of causal diagrams?
    1. _____
    2. _____

26.   What is wrong with the following causal diagrams?

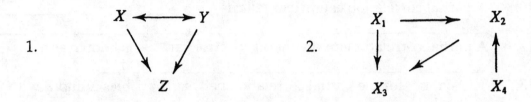

27.   The statistical method for testing causal models is called _____.
28.   In causal models, what are residual values?

_____

_____

REVIEW TESTS

Multiple-Choice   Place the letter corresponding to the one BEST answer in the space provided.

_____ 1.   In quasi-experimental research design, techniques of control:
     a.   involve separation of subjects into experimental and control groups
     b.   are statistical methods used during the data analysis stage of the research
     c.   are employed during the data-collection stage of the research
     d.   are useless for determining the spuriousness of bivariate relationships

_____ 2.   Which of these is NOT a method of control used in quasi-experimental research?
     a.   factor analysis
     b.   cross-tabulation
     c.   partial correlation
     d.   multiple regression

_____ 3.	In using the cross-tabulation method of control, the variable the researcher has identified as the control variable must be:
	a.	related to the dependent variable but not to the independent variable
	b.	related only to the independent variable
	c.	related to both the independent and dependent variables
	d.	unrelated to both the independent and dependent variables

_____ 4.	If, after controlling for a third variable, we find that the original bivariate relationship is unchanged, we can conclude that the:
	a.	original relationship is spurious
	b.	original relationship is nonspurious
	c.	independent variable is the cause of the dependent variable
	d.	control variable is related to the independent variable but not to the dependent variable

_____ 5.	As a method of control, cross-tabulation is applicable to:
	a.	nominal variables
	b.	ordinal variables
	c.	interval variables
	d.	all levels of measurement

_____ 6.	Elaboration involves:
	a.	demonstrating that a bivariate relationship is spurious
	b.	introducing control variables to determine the conditions under which an original bivariate relationship occurs
	c.	isolating the one independent variable that does the best job of explaining a dependent variable
	d.	converting b coefficients into beta weights

_____ 7.	In the scheme: Education, Income, Political Party Affiliation, Income is:
	a.	the dependent variable
	b.	a conditional variable
	c.	an intervening variable
	d.	an extraneous variable

_____ 8.   A disadvantage of cross-tabulation is that it:
   a.   requires relatively large samples
   b.   is restricted to the use of only one control variable
   c.   cannot be used to determine spuriousness
   d.   is restricted to the use of interval variables

_____ 9.   In contrast to cross-tabulation, partial correlation:
   a.   can be used to show the cause-effect nature of a bivariate relationship
   b.   produces a summary statistic of the amount of correlation between two variables controlling for the effects of a third variable
   c.   requires nominal or ordinal variables
   d.   requires samples of 200 or more

_____ 10.   Which of the following expresses a first-order partial?
   a. $r_{13.2}$
   b. $r_{23.2}$
   c. $r_{12.3}$
   d. $r_{23.1}$

_____ 11.   What three elements of information are needed to compute the beta weight for an independent variable X?
   a.   the mean of X, the standard deviation of the dependent variable, Y, and the bivariate correlation of X and Y
   b.   the standard deviation of X, the standard deviation of Y, and the bivariate correlation of X and Y
   c.   the standard deviation of X, the standard deviation of Y, and the partial regression, b, of X
   d.   the intercept, a, the bivariate correlation of X and Y, and the partial regression, b of X

_____ 12.   Suppose we obtained the following multiple regression equation which has a good fit to the data:

$$Y = 12.6 + 3X_1 + X_2$$

If $X_1 = 2/4$ and $X_2 = 6.3$, the predicted value of Y would be:
a.   12.6
b.   13.5
c.   26.1
d.   Y cannot be determined on the basis of the information give.

_____ 13.   The statistic that expresses the combined effect of several independent variables on a dependent variable is the:
a.   coefficient of determination
b.   _b_ coefficient
c.   beta weight
d.   partial correlation

_____ 14.   Which of the following diagrams violates the simplifying assumptions of causal models?

a.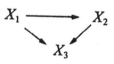

b.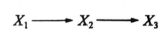

c.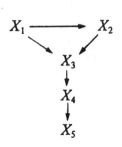

d.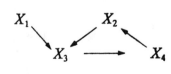

_____ 15.   Consider the following causal model:

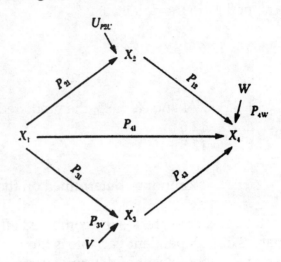

The term W signifies
a.   the bivariate correlations of X_3 with X_1 and X_2 respectively
b.   the combined effects of X_1 and X_2 on X_3
c.   the combined effects of X_1, X_2, and X_3 on X_4
d.   the variation in X_4 unaccounted for by X_1, X_2, and X_3

True-False   Circle T is the answer is true, F if it is false.

T   F   1.   If we find that two variables are highly correlated, we can infer that one causes the other.

T   F   2.   If after introducing a third variable we find that the original bivariate correlation is maintained, we can conclude that the relationship is nonspurious.

T   F   3.   An advantage cross-tabulation has over other methods of control is that it is unaffected by sample size.

T   F   4.   Many conditional factors are associated with almost any two-variable relationship.

T   F   5.   The partial correlation coefficient reflects the amount of correlation between an independent variable and two dependent variables.

T   F   6.   A second-order partial reflects the amount of correlation between an independent variable and two dependent variables.

T   F   7.   In the regression equation $Y = a + b_1X_1 + b_2X_1$, the term b_1X_1 stands for the amount of change in Y produced by a unit change in X_1 with X_2 held constant.

T   F   8.   In multiple regression, the point where the regression line crosses the Y axis is called the beta weight.

T   F   9.   In most instances beta weights and partial correlations for the same variables will have opposite signs.

T   F   10.   Elaboration involves determining the conditions under which a given bivariate relationship holds.

T   F   11.   Distinguishing between spurious and intervening interpretations of the effects of a third variable is largely a statistical issue.

T   F   12.   The coefficient of determination reflects the amount of variation in a dependent variable accounted for by several independent variables.

T   F   13.   A coefficient of determination of .50 means that independent variables in a multiple regression equation account for half of the variation in the dependent variable.

T   F   14.   In causal modeling, a path coefficient of zero means no direct link exists between the two variables concerned.

T   F   15.   Residual variables in a causal model express variation that exists within the model's dependent variables.

EXERCISES AND PROJECTS

Exercise 17-1

Study the following bivariate and partial tables.

Table 17a.   **RACE AND VOTER TURNOUT**

	RACE	
	African American	**White**
Voted	44%	62%
Did not vote	56%	38%
	(200)	(450)

Table 17b.   **RACE AND VOTER TURNOUT BY EDUCATION**

EDUCATION LEVEL

	College Graduates		**Non-College Graduates**	
	African American	**White**	**African American**	**White**
Voted	68%	73%	29%	33%
Did not vote	32%	27%	71%	67%
	(100)	(250)	(200)	(150)

In the space below, interpret the effects of education on the original relationship between race and voter turnout.

Exercise 17-2

Determine the partial correlation between X and Y with z held constant (controlled), then the partial correlation between Y and z with X held constant, using the following zero-order bivariate correlations: $r_{xy} = .40$, $r_{xz} = .30$, $r_{zy} = .10$

1. $r_{xy.z} =$ _____

2. $r_{yz.x} =$ _____

Exercise 17-3

Write a set of equations in general form to describe each of the following causal systems, assuming that X_1 is the independent variable, X_2 and X_3 are intervening variables, and X_4 is the dependent variable.

Model 1:

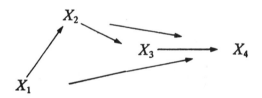

Model 2:

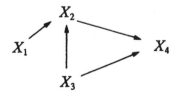

Exercise 17-4

Use the following trivariate table to determine whether there is a relationship between religion and attitudes toward premarital sex. If there is a relationship, determine if and how the third variable, age, affects this relationship. Note that you will first have to collapse the table into a bivariate table to discover the relationship between religion and attitudes toward premarital sex. Then you can use the trivariate table to examine the effects of the third variable.

		AGE			
		Under-40		40 and over	
		Protestant	Catholic	Protestant	Catholic
Attitude Toward Premarital Sex	Approve	220	110	30	60
	Disapprove	180	90	270	540
	Total	400	200	300	600

CHAPTER 18

INDEX CONSTRUCTION

AND SCALING METHODS

CHAPTER ABSTRACT

In this chapter, we first discuss the logic of index construction and present several techniques for constructing indexes. Next, we discuss the Likert scaling technique, which measures attitudes on the ordinal and the interval levels of measurement. Then, we present and illustrate Guttman scaling, or scalogram analysis, as a method for scaling. The Guttman technique can be applied to nominal and ordinal levels of analysis.

CHAPTER OBJECTIVES

After studying this chapter, you should be able to:

1.   explain the differences between a scale and an index.

2.   construct a simple index.

3.   describe the process of constructing Likert and Guttman scales, and explain factor analysis.

MAIN POINTS

Introduction

Many concepts employed in the social sciences are complex and difficult to measure with single indicators. Indexes and scales are composite measures constructed through the combination of two or more items or indicators. Indexes usually involve adding together measurements from single indicators; scales are more carefully constructed in an attempt to ensure that only one dimension is measured.

Index Construction

The combination of two or more items or indicators yields an index. Four major problems are involved in constructing indexes: definition of purpose for which the index is being compiled, selection and collection of sources of data, selection of the base comparison, and selection of methods of aggregation and weighting. Attitude indexes, also referred to as arbitrary scales, involve a battery of questions that are selected on an a priori basis.

Scaling Methods

Likert scaling is a method designed to measure people's attitudes. Six steps can be distinguished in the construction of a Likert scale: 1) compiling possible scale items, 2) administering items to a random sample of respondents, 3) computing a total score for each respondent, 4) determining the discriminative power (DP) of items, 5) selecting the scale items, and 6) testing reliability.

Guttman scaling is designed to incorporate an empirical test of the unidimensionality of a set of items as an integral part of the scale-construction process. Guttman scales are unidimensional as well as cumulative. In practice, a perfect Guttman scale is rarely obtainable; consequently, Guttman developed a criterion for evaluating the unidimensional and cumulative assumptions: the coefficient of reproducibility (CR), which measures the degree of conformity to a perfect scalable pattern. There are four major steps in constructing a Guttman scale: 1) selecting scale items, 2) recording responses on a scalogram sheet, 3) calculating the coefficient of reproducibility, and 4) refining the scale.

Factor analysis is a statistical technique for classifying a large number of interrelated variables into a smaller number of dimensions or factors. It is a useful method for the construction of multiple-item scales, where each scale represents a dimension of a more abstract construct. First, bivariate correlations are computed, and then these correlations are placed in a matrix format. The correlation matrix is used as the input data in the factor analysis procedure. Finally, a composite scale is developed for each factor.

KEY TERMS (page reference in parenthesis)
To assist you in familiarizing yourself with the Key Terms, imagine a series of "short answer" questions that ask you to define each term in your own words, using the text's discussion as a guide.

coefficient of
reproducibility (426)
discriminative power (424)
factor analysis (427)

factor score coefficient (430)
Guttman scale (425)
index (415)
item (414)

Likert scale (422)
simple aggregate (418)
unidimensionality (415)
weighted aggregate (419)

SELF-EVALUATION EXERCISES

Introduction

1.   Indexes and scales are extensions of issues of _____.
2.   Indexes and scales are constructed by combining two or more _____ of a concept.
3.   Three reasons for using indexes and scales in the social sciences are:
     1.   _____
     2.   _____
     3.   _____
4.   How do scales differ from indexes?

     _____
     _____
     _____

Index Construction

5.   Four problems are involved in constructing indexes. These are:
     1.   _____
     2.   _____
     3.   _____
     4.   _____
6.   In constructing indexes, how do weighted aggregates differ from simple aggregates?

     _____
     _____
     _____

7.   What is "arbitrary" about arbitrary scales?

_____

_____

_____

Scaling Methods

8.   Likert scaling is a common method for measuring _____.

9.   The six steps involved in constructing a Likert scale are:

1.   _____

2.   _____

3.   _____

4.   _____

5.   _____

6.   _____

10.   Guttman scales are both _____ and _____.

11.   A measure of the extent to which a scale pattern approaches a perfect Guttman scale is known as the _____.

12.   If you had constructed a scale wherein there were 126 "errors" (inconsistencies) among 840 responses, the coefficient of reproducibility would be

        _____.

13.   The purpose of factor analysis is to _____

_____

_____

_____.

14.   The correlation between an individual variable and a factor is called a

        _____.

REVIEW TESTS

Multiple-Choice   Place the letter corresponding to the one BEST answer in the space provided.

_____   1.   Which of the following is NOT a reason for using indexes and scales?
                 a.   to produce more reliable measurements
                 b.   to reduce the complexity of data
                 c.   to provide representative samples
                 d.   to provide measures that are more precise and amenable to statistical manipulation

_____ 2.   Indexes and scales differ in that:
    a.   indexes are more complicated
    b.   scales are more carefully constructed
    c.   indexes are more valid and scales are more reliable
    d.   scales involve weighted aggregation

_____ 3.   Weighted aggregation is preferable to simple aggregation when:
    a.   a Guttman scale is being constructed
    b.   the individual indicators are of differing importance
    c.   an index involves more than 10 indicators
    d.   economic indexes are being constructed

_____ 4.   The major objective in using a Likert scale is to:
    a.   end up with a measure comprised of at least 20 items
    b.   identify the one indicator which best represents the concept the researcher wishes to measure
    c.   ensure that all items tap the same dimension of the concept the researcher wishes to measure
    d.   prevent respondents from figuring out the intent of the research

_____ 5.   In Likert scaling, item analysis is a method for:
    a.   determining the discriminative power of items
    b.   determining the appropriate size of the sample of respondents
    c.   computing the coefficient of reliability
    d.   determining the number of response categories to assign to individual items

_____ 6.   In a track meet a pole vaulter consistently vaults 20 feet. Keeping in mind the principles of Guttman scaling, we can assume that the same pole vaulter could:
    a.   vault 21 feet
    b.   vault 20 feet in his next meet
    c.   vault 19 feet
    d.   throw a shot-put 20 feet

_____ 7.   If a Guttman scale yields a coefficient of reproducibility of .50, we can conclude that the scale is:
        a.   reliable but not valid
        b.   valid but not reliable
        c.   cumulative
        d.   not cumulative

_____ 8.   One of the simplest statistics to examine in order to determine which items to retain in a scale and which items to discard is:
        a.   multiple regressions
        b.   nonparametric measures
        c.   probabilistic inferences
        d.   bivariate correlations

_____ 9.   Factor analysis is used to:
        a.   discover basic patterns of interrelationships among variables
        b.   determine the consistency of responses among variables
        c.   redefine variables as a single concept
        d.   measure the discriminative power of Likert scale items

_____ 10.   The results of factor analysis that would display the statistical relationship between each variable and its underlying factor are called:
        a.   dimensions
        b.   Pearson correlations
        c.   factor matrices
        d.   factor loadings

True-False   Circle T is the answer is true, F if it is false.

T   F   1.   Scales are generally more rigorous than indexes in their construction.

T   F   2.   The main difference between arbitrary scales and Likert scale has to do with the number of items in each.

T   F   3.   Attitude indexes are sometimes called arbitrary scales because they do not involve procedures for determining the internal consistency of items.

T   F   4.   To construct a Likert scale, one begins by determining its reliability.

T   F   5.   Total scores on Likert scales are computed by adding together the responses to all of the individual items that are checked.

T   F   6.   Perfect Guttman scales, though difficult to construct, are relatively common in the social sciences.

T   F   7.   A coefficient of reproducibility of .90 would indicate that a Guttman scale is multidimensional.

T   F   8.   In a Guttman scale, the coefficient of reproducibility measures the deviation between actual responses and a pattern of perfectly consistent responses.

T   F   9.   Factor analysis is used to classify a large number of variables into a smaller number of dimensions.

T   F   10.   In factor analysis, variables with the lowest factor loadings are the ones that are the best indicators of the factor.

EXERCISES AND PROJECTS

Exercises 18-1

Using the accompanying table, which gives values for a hypothetical violent crime index, shift the base from 1972 to 1992 and recalculate values for each of the years in the table.

Year	Index of Violent Crime (1972 = 100)	Index of Violent Crime (1992 = 100)
1964	96.8	_____
1968	100.4	_____
1972	100.0	_____
1976	104.2	_____

Year	Index of Violent Crime (1972 = 100)	Index of Violent Crime (1992 = 100)
1980	116.8	_____
1988	132.5	_____
1992	140.0	<u>100.0</u>
1996	138.6 (est)	_____

Exercise 18-2

Assume that we wish to construct an index of community integration involving the following indicators:

   a.   Whether a person owns a home
   b.   Whether a person is married
   c.   Whether a person has children in community schools
   d.   Whether a person belongs to community organizations
   e.   Whether a person has lived in the community for more than 10 years

In this index, indicators *a*, *b*, and *c* are to be weighted equally, *d* is to be given triple weight, and *e* is to be given double weight. A person receives a 1 if he or she answers yes to the question and a 0 otherwise.

   1.   What is the minimum value a person can achieve on the index?
        _____

   2.   What is the maximum value a person can achieve on the index?
        _____

   3.   What score would a person receive who is single, owns a home, has no children, belongs to several community organizations, and has lived in the community for 5 years? _____

   4.   What score would a person receive who is married, rents an apartment, has two children in community schools, has lived in the community for 12 years, and belongs to no community organizations? _____

   5.   What score would a person receive who is married, owns a home, has a child in community schools, belongs to one community organization, and has lived in the community for 2 years? _____

Exercise 18-3

Write a set of five items to measure a concept of your choice. These items should be such that they are likely to constitute a Guttman scale. In other words, the items should be increasingly difficult or restrictive so that a respondent who "passes" an item will also be very likely to "pass" all scale items that are "easier."

What concept are you trying to measure? _____

List the items in order of increasing difficulty or restrictiveness.

    1.   (Least difficult) _____

    2.   _____

    3.   _____

    4.   _____

    5.   (Most difficult) _____

Exercise 18-4

The following data responses are given by twenty people to a 6-item scale. The response alternatives to each of the items range from 1 (strongly disagree) to 5 (strongly agree). Your task is to (1) calculate a total score for each person; (2) arrange the responses on a scalogram sheet (which you will have to make yourself); (3) determine proper cut points; (4) calculate the coefficient of reproducibility; (5) indicate whether this constitutes a Guttman scale.

Person	Item 1	Item 2	Item 3	Item 4	Item 5	Item 6	Total
A	5	5	4	4	4	2	_____
B	5	5	4	4	3	2	_____
C	5	5	2	2	2	1	_____
D	4	3	1	2	1	1	_____
E	4	3	1	2	1	1	_____
F	4	4	4	3	3	2	_____
G	5	5	4	4	4	2	_____
H	5	4	4	3	3	2	_____
I	5	4	3	2	2	1	_____
J	5	4	3	3	2	2	_____
K	5	4	3	3	2	2	_____
L	4	3	2	2	2	1	_____
M	4	4	2	2	2	1	_____
N	5	5	4	4	3	2	_____
O	5	3	4	5	3	2	_____
P	4	5	3	5	3	2	_____

Person	Item 1	Item 2	Item 3	Item 4	Item 5	Item 6	Total
Q	5	5	4	3	3	2	_____
R	5	4	2	2	2	1	_____
S	4	3	1	2	1	2	_____
T	2	2	2	2	1	1	_____

Exercise 18-5

Devise at least six items that could be used to measure the concept of "job satisfaction."
Show how the responses to these items would be scored and how they could be
combined into an index.

Exercise 18-6

Write 10 items that could be used in a Likert scale to measure attitudes toward the concept of regional government (as opposed to traditional city and county government). Be sure the items are clear, grammatically correct, and appear to measure the same dimension. Provide an appropriate set of 5-point alternatives for each question.

Exercise 18-7

In a study of political participation, you ask a sample of 100 persons the following four questions:

Item 1:	Have you ever run for public office?
Item 2:	In the past year have you attended political rallies or meetings?
Item 3:	In the most recent election did you ever persuade others to vote a certain way?
Item 4:	Did you vote in the last election?

Responses to these items produced the following results:

Item 1	Item 2	Item 3	Item 4	Number of Respondents
Yes	Yes	Yes	Yes	2
No	Yes	Yes	Yes	10
No	No	Yes	Yes	15

Item 1	Item 2	Item 3	Item 4	Number of Respondents
No	No	No	Yes	25
No	No	No	No	40
No	Yes	No	No	4
No	Yes	No	Yes	2
Yes	No	Yes	Yes	2

Step 1.   Compute the coefficient of reproducibility for these data.

Step 2.   What does the coefficient of reproducibility tell you about the four items?

Step 3.   Which of the four items would you eliminate in order to increase the coefficient of reproducibility?

Step 4.   If you eliminated this item, what would the new coefficient of reproducibility be?

CHAPTER 19

INFERENCES

CHAPTER ABSTRACT

In this chapter, we describe the strategy of hypothesis testing by focusing on such concepts as: sampling distribution, Type I and Type II errors, and the level of significance. We then consider several methods of testing hypotheses about the relationship between two variables: difference between means, Pearson's r, and the chi-square test.

CHAPTER OBJECTIVES

After studying this chapter, you should be able to:

1.   describe the process of hypothesis testing.

2.   distinguish between research and null hypotheses.

3.   distinguish between one- and two-tailed tests and between Type I and Type II errors.

4.   conduct significance tests for the difference between means and correlations.

5.   identify the distinctive characteristics of parametric and nonparametric tests of significance.

6.   conduct the chi-square test of significance.

MAIN POINTS

Introduction

Statistical inference enables investigators to evaluate the accuracy of their estimates. A second use of inferential statistics is in the assessment of the probability of specific sample results under assumed population conditions. This type of inferential statistics is called hypothesis testing. It leads to the determination of whether sample results characterize the population as a whole or reflect chance occurrences.

The Strategy of Testing Hypotheses

The first step in testing a hypothesis is to formulate it in statistical terms. This procedure involves the following steps:

1.   Formulate a null hypothesis and a research hypothesis.
2.   Choose a sampling distribution and a statistical test according to the null hypothesis.
3.   Specify a significance level and define the region of rejection.
4.   Compute the statistical test, and reject or retain the null hypothesis accordingly.

Null and Research Hypotheses

There are two statistical hypotheses involved in the process of testing hypotheses: the research hypothesis and the null hypothesis. The need for two hypotheses arises out of a logical necessity: the null hypothesis is based on negative inference in order to avoid the fallacy of affirming the consequent--that is, researchers must eliminate false hypotheses rather than accept true ones. Support for a research hypothesis is provided by data that lead to rejection of a null hypothesis.

Sampling Distribution

Having formulated a specific null hypothesis, the investigator proceeds to test it against the sample result. In order to determine the accuracy of the sample statistic, one has to compare it to a statistical model that gives the probability of observing such a result. Such a statistical model is called a sampling distribution and is the theoretical distribution that would result if all possible samples of a given size were drawn and then a statistic (such as a mean, a proportion, or a correlation) were calculated on each sample and arrayed in a frequency distribution. Such a distribution is used, in combination with probability theory, to determine how likely it is that a given sample statistic (the one calculated on the sample actually dealt with) is atypical.

Level of Significance and Region of Rejection

The range of the results in a sampling distribution that are very unlikely to occur is referred to as the region of rejection. The sum of the probabilities of the results included in the region of rejection is denoted as the level of significance. If a calculated statistic is so extreme that it falls in the region of rejection on a sampling distribution, then the researcher rejects the null hypothesis and assumes that the sample result is real rather than due to chance.

A statistical test may be one-tailed or two-tailed. In testing a directional research hypothesis, a one-tailed test should be used. This means that the region of rejection for the null hypothesis falls at only one end of the sampling distribution. In testing a nondirectional research hypothesis, a two-tailed test should be used.

A Type I error occurs when a true null hypothesis is rejected. A Type II error occurs when a null hypothesis that is actually false is accepted. The likelihood of a Type I error can be directly controlled because it is determined by the level of significance (alpha) that is utilized.

Parametric and Nonparametric Tests of Significance

Parametric tests of significance are based on assumptions about the parameters of the population from which the sample is drawn. Nonparametric statistical tests are used when such assumptions about population characteristics cannot be reasonably made. There are certain assumptions associated with most nonparametric tests; however, they are weaker and fewer than those associated with parametric tests.

Parametric tests include the difference-between-means test. When the dependent variable being investigated is measured on an interval scale, a comparison of means can be used to reflect the amount of relationship between two variables. The t test is used to test for the significance of differences between sample means. This type of test is used to examine a research hypothesis that the average value of some particular variable differs in two different groups in a population (such as male and female, urban and rural dwellers, etc.). A similar t test can be conducted in order to test a research hypothesis that two variables are correlated in a population.

The chi-square test is a nonparametric test used to test the hypothesis that a dependent variable is distributed differently within various conditions of an independent variable. Thus, it provides a significance test of the relationship between the two variables in the population.

KEY TERMS (page reference in parenthesis)
To assist you in familiarizing yourself with the Key Terms, imagine a series of "short answer" questions that ask you to define each term in your own words, using the text's discussion as a guide.

chi-square test (450)	nonparametric tests (444)	sampling distribution (439)
degrees of	null hypothesis (438)	*t* test (447)
freedom (df) (447)	one-tailed test (442)	two-tailed test (442)
difference-between-	parametric test (444)	Type I error (443)
means test (444)	region of rejection (440)	Type II error (443)
level of significance (440)	research hypothesis (438)	

SELF-EVALUATION EXERCISES

Introduction

1. The use of statistics to assess the probability of certain sample results, given a particular population, is known as

    _____.

The Strategy of Testing Hypotheses

2. The first step in testing a hypothesis is to

    _____.

Null and Research Hypotheses

3. The null hypothesis is usually symbolized as _____.
4. The null hypothesis is the _____ of the research hypothesis.
5. Briefly explain what is meant by the fallacy of affirming the consequent.

    _____

    _____

Sampling Distribution

6. A statistical model that gives the probability of a given sample is called a

    _____.

Level of Significance and Region of Rejection

7.   The range of probabilities that would result in rejection of the null hypothesis is the _____.

8.   The sum of the probabilities in the region of rejection is known as the

_____.

9.   With a significance level of .05, one rejects a null hypothesis if, as an empirical result, it would have occurred by chance no more than _____ percent of the time.

10.   If the region of rejection is located only at one end of the sampling distribution, one is conducting a _____ test.

11.   If the direction of a research hypothesis cannot accurately be predicted, one must conduct a _____ test.

12.   Rejecting a null hypothesis that is actually true is known as a _____ error; accepting a null hypothesis that is false is a _____ error.

13.   The level of significance is the _____.

14.   As one increases the likelihood of making a Type I error, one _____ (increases/decreases) the likelihood of making a Type II error.

15.   The most commonly used significance levels in the social sciences are

_____, _____, and _____.

Parametric and Nonparametric Tests of Significance

16.   A statistical test that is based on a number of assumptions about population characteristics is called a(n) _____.

17.   Give the major assumptions that are necessary to conduct a parametric test of significance.

        1.   _____

        2.   _____

18.   A statistical test that does not require the assumptions referred to in the previous questions is called a _____ test.

19.   Give the symbolic representation of a null hypothesis to indicate no difference between means of groups 2 and 3. _____

20.   The normal distribution can be used as a sampling distribution to test the difference between means when _____

_____.

21.   It is necessary to use the *t* distribution as one's sampling distribution when

_____.

22.   What is the critical value of t (the value for which the null hypothesis will be rejected) in each of the following instances?

Test	Significance Level	n_1	n_2	Critical t Value
One-tailed	1	22	10	_____
Two-tailed	.05	6	10	_____
One-tailed	.005	12	12	_____
Two-tailed	.01	14	10	_____
One-tailed	.05	18	24	_____

23.   Use a t test on the following sample data to test the research hypothesis that the average age of female undergraduates is less than the average age of male undergraduates. Use the .05 level of significance, and state the null and research hypotheses symbolically.

	Males	Females
X	21.84	21.32
s^2	1.20	.84
n	25	16

24.   If we have discovered a correlation of .36 in a sample of 85 persons, is it possible to reject the null hypothesis (that there is no correlation in the population) at the .05 level of significance? If so, why?

_____

_____

_____

25.   Use a significance test for Pearson's r to test the research hypothesis that rho (the population correlation) is greater than .50, based on a sample of size 39 which yields an r of .58. (Use the .05 level of significance.)

Your result: _____

26.   Test the hypothesis that the population correlation is less than .40, based on a sample of 124 persons which provides a correlation of .26. (Use the .05 level of significance.)

Your result: _____

27.   Use the following ordinal-level data to test the research hypothesis that Republicans are more likely than Democrats to be rated favorably by the Moral Majority. The data represent ratings on a scale from 1. to 100. (Use the .05 level of significance.)

Republicans		Democrats	
Person	Rating	Person	Rating
A	100	G	62
B	88	H	4
C	93	I	81
D	75	J	58
E	61	K	70

Republicans		Democrats	
Person	Rating	Person	Rating
F	14	L	8
M	47		
N	2		
O	10		

Your results: _____

28.   The chi-square test is most commonly applied to a situation wherein _____.

29.   The number of degrees of freedom for a chi-square test on a table with 4 rows and 5 columns would be _____.

30.   Use the following data to test the null hypothesis that political affiliation and voting intentions are not related. (Use the .01 level of significance.)

Voting Intention	Political Affiliation		
	Democrat	Republican	Independent
Democrat	34	5	24
Republican	3	21	10
Third-party candidate	23	4	36

Your results: _____

REVIEW TESTS

Multiple-Choice   Place the letter corresponding to the one BEST answer in the space provided.

_____ 1.   In order to provide support for a hypothesis, one must:
      a.   affirm the consequent
      b.   use very large samples
      c.   reject the null hypothesis
      d.   accept the null hypothesis

_____ 2.   The _____ hypothesis states that there is no statistically significant association between two variables.
      a.   research
      b.   bivariate
      c.   null
      d.   rival

_____ 3.   If a research hypothesis predicts that juvenile delinquency rates are higher among only children than among children with siblings, the null hypothesis would predict that:
      a.   there is no difference between only children and siblings with regard to juvenile delinquency
      b.   the relationship between juvenile delinquency and number of siblings is negative
      c.   juvenile delinquency is higher among children with siblings
      d.   the relationship between delinquency and number of siblings is unknown

_____ 4.   If a research hypothesis predicts that off-campus college students have lower grade-point averages than the general college population, what kind of test of significance should be used?
      a.   a right-tailed test
      b.   a left-tailed test
      c.   a two-tailed test
      d.   standard deviation

_____ 5.   The probability of committing a Type I error and rejecting a true hypothesis is:
      a.   the same as the probability of making a Type II error
      b.   greater when parametric measures are employed
      c.   .50 or greater
      d.   equivalent to the level of significance

_____ 6.   A Type II error involves:
      a.   rejecting a true research hypothesis
      b.   rejecting a true null hypothesis
      c.   accepting a true research hypothesis
      d.   failing to accept a true null hypothesis

_____ 7.   A sampling distribution refers to:
      a.   all elements in a sample
      b.   a number of samples
      c.   a set of sampling methods
      d.   a theoretical distribution of sample statistics

_____ 8.   Which of the following is true of a directional research hypothesis?
      a.   It must be accompanied by a directional null hypothesis.
      b.   It can be tested only with a two-tailed test.
      c.   It involves affirming the consequent.
      d.   It utilizes a split critical region.

_____ 9.   To test the hypothesis that age and political activism are correlated in the U.S. population, one could draw a probability sample, determine the correlation between the two variables in the sample, and then do a:
      a.   chi-square test on age
      b.   Mann-Whitney test on political activism
      c. t test of mean differences between age and activism
      d. t test on the correlation between age and activism

_____ 10.   Of the following, only the _____ is a parametric test of significance.
      a. t test
      b.   chi-square test
      c.   Mann-Whitney test on political activism
      d. t test on correlation between age and activism

_____ 11.   In a chi-square test, the degrees of freedom in a table with six rows and four columns would be:
  a.   1
  b.   10
  c.   15
  d.   24

_____ 12.   In the chi-square test of significance, the "expected" frequencies are those that would be expected assuming there is:
  a.   a strong relationship between two variables
  b.   no relationship between two variables
  c.   a positive relationship between two variables
  d.   a negative relationship between two variables

_____ 13.   In the computation of chi-square, a level of significance of .02 means there is:
  a.   a 98 percent likelihood that the sample is representative of the population
  b.   a 2 percent probability that a given chi-square value could have been obtained due to chance
  c.   a 98 percent probability that a given chi-square value could have been obtained due to chance
  d.   no association between two variables

_____ 14.   In a bivariate table, the minimum number of cells whose frequencies we would need to know in order to determine the frequencies in the remaining cells is known as:
  a.   chi-square
  b.   level of significance
  c.   degrees of freedom
  d.   region of rejection

_____ 15.   The _F_ statistic is a test of significance used in association with:
  a.   Pearson's _r_
  b.   chi-square
  c.   the _t_ distribution
  d.   the Mann-Whitney test

True-False   Circle T if the answer is true, F if it is false.

T   F   1.   The procedure of a statistical inference allows a researcher to determine whether sample results are likely to have occurred by chance.

T   F   2.   A hypothesis test actually involves two hypothesis

T   F   3.   The null hypothesis is usually of no difference or no relationship between variables.

T   F   4.   Statistical tests are used to test the research hypothesis only.

T   F   5.   The credibility of an explanation can be established only by eliminating competing explanations of a phenomenon.

T   F   6.   If a research hypothesis specifies that a sample mean is likely to be higher than the mean of a given population, a right-tailed test should be used.

T   F   7.   Sampling distributions can be constructed for means and proportions but not for variances.

T   F   8.   A researcher who uses the .05 level of significance will falsely reject a true hypothesis 95 percent of the time.

T   F   9.   A statistical test that allows one to reject a null hypothesis provides proof that it is incorrect.

T   F   10.   Type II errors are less serious than Type I errors.

T   F   11.   A finding that is substantially significant is always statistically significant as well.

T   F   12.   Parametric tests permit variables of any level of measurement.

T   F   13.   Chi-square is most often employed for determining whether a significant relationship exists between two nominal variables.

T   F   14.   The concept of degrees of freedom refers to the number of free choices one can make in repeated samples that constitute sampling distributions.

EXERCISES AND PROJECTS

Exercise 19-1

You are doing a study in which you are investigating the research hypothesis that approval of government welfare programs for the poor is related to political party identification. A sample survey of 100 respondents has yielded the following observations:

Attitude Toward Welfare Programs	Political Affiliation		
	Democrat	Republican	Independent
Approve	17	11	12
Disapprove	8	24	8

1.   State the null hypothesis.

2.   Based on the observations, compute the expected frequencies and enter them in the following table.

Attitude Toward Welfare Programs	Political Affiliation		
	Democrat	Republican	Independent
Approve			
Disapprove			

3.   Compute the value of chi-square.

4.   How many degrees of freedom are there?

5.   At what levels of significance can the null hypothesis be rejected?

ANSWER KEY

CHAPTER 1

Self-Evaluation Exercises

1. methodology
2. "to know"
3. logical reasoning
4. none. Mystical knowledge consists of manifestations of supernatural signs.
5. rationalistic
6. F
7. tautological
8. F
9. natural phenomena have natural causes
10. nothing is self-evident
11. senses
12. explanation, prediction; sense of understanding
13. deductive
14. express the relationships between variables as tendencies rather than as absolutes
15. certain conclusions cannot be drawn about a particular unit within a whole set of units
16. *Verstehen*; interpretive
17. scientific methodology
18. logic
19. empirical fact
20. intersubjectivity
21. logic
22. Normal science
23. anomalies
24. scientific revolution
25. context of discovery
26. logical; empirical
27. Problems lead to empirical research; research in turn leads to new problems; and so on.
28. It is capable of detecting not only invalid conclusions and generalizations but also defects in the performance of research operations.
29. F
30. F

Multiple-Choice Questions

1.   b
2.   c
3.   c
4.   a
5.   d
6.   b
7.   a
8.   c
9.   c
10. d
11. a
12. b
13. c
14. a
15. a
16. a
17. c
18. d

True-False Questions

1.   F
2.   F
3.   T
4.   T
5.   F
6.   F
7.   T
8.   F
9.   T
10. F

CHAPTER 2

Self-Evaluation Exercises

1.   abstractions
2.   fish
3.   social organization
4.   reification
5.   structure
6.   theories
7.   conceptual
8.   primitive
9.   primitive
10. operational
11. theoretical
12. practice
13. philosophy; theory

14. (1) ad hoc classificatory system; (2) taxonomies; (3) conceptual frameworks; (4) theoretical systems
15. (1) They specify the units of empirical reality and indicate how they may be described. (2) They summarize and inspire descriptive studies.
16. explanations; predictions
17. (1) general scope; (2) set of concepts; (3) set of propositions; (4) a calculus (rules for deducing propositions); (5) contingency of propositions
18. (1) set of concepts and definitions; (2) set of existence statements; (3) set of relational statements, axioms, and theorems; (4) logical system relating all concepts and deducing theorems
19. size (or parsimony)
20. causal
21. (1) clear descriptiveness; (2) conceptual clarity; (3) parsimony; (4) integration of propositions; (5) axiom examination; (6) compatibility with causal analysis
22. simplifying
23. abstractions (or representations)
24. theory, research
25. (1) selecting phenomena; (2) measuring phenomena; (3) analyzing data; (4) discovering patterns (constructing theory)
26. (1) j; (2) a; (3) h; (4) f; (5) i; (6) e; (7) g; (8) l or g

Multiple-Choice Questions		*True-False Questions*	
1.	b	1.	T
2.	c	2.	T
3.	b	3.	F
4.	b	4.	F
5.	a	5.	F
6.	b	6.	F
7.	d	7.	T
8.	d	8.	F
9.	c	9.	F
10.	a	10.	F
11.	a		
12.	b		
13.	a		
14.	b		
15.	d		

CHAPTER 3

Self-Evaluation Exercises

1. problem
2. empirical research
3. the things (entities) to which concepts pertain
4. persons
5. the individualistic fallacy
6. the country is a democracy
7. communists are the perpetrators of violence
8. A concept is an abstraction. When the abstraction is converted into a property with a number of different values, it is a variable.
9. independent variable; dependent variable
10. You may be interested in explaining a phenomenon such as auto accidents, in which case auto accidents are the dependent variable. On the other hand, you would consider auto accidents the *independent variable* if you wanted to see what effect they had on some other variable (such as attitudes toward safety regulations).
11. spurious
12. Continuous variables can be broken down into successively smaller units to the limits of our ability to measure small differences. Discrete variables can be broken down only to some indivisible unit and no further.
13. variables
14. change together and have something in common
15. positive
16. decreases
17. magnitude
18. perfect; zero
19. Problems pose questions for research. Hypotheses are tentative answers to research problems.
20. (1) clear; (2) value-free; (3) specific; (4) testable with available methods
21. 1, 4, 5
22. It is not specific enough. The hypothesis should assert how Democrats and Republicans are expected to differ in their opinions on foreign aid.
23. journals
24. brief summaries of the research cited

Multiple-Choice Questions		*True-False Questions*	
1.	a	1.	F
2.	c	2.	F
3.	d	3.	T
4.	c	4.	F
5.	a	5.	T
6.	d	6.	F
7.	c	7.	F
8.	b	8.	T
9.	b	9.	T
10.	c	10.	F
11.	c	11.	F
12.	a	12.	T
13.	b	13.	F
14.	c	14.	T
15.	d		

CHAPTER 4

Self-Evaluation Exercises

1. ethics
2. (1) There may have been deception. (2) Participants may have suffered stress. (3) The experiment may have caused participants to distrust authorities in the future. (4) The participants received no apparent benefit from participating in the study.
3. He used deception to do the study. The individuals studied did not volunteer for the study actually conducted, but rather for the one they were led to believe was to be done. Such studies may produce a general distrust of researchers and prevent useful research from being done in the future.
4. confidentiality
5. it has practical and methodological advantages
6. (1) the right or researchers and the general public to research and knowledge; (2) the right of research participants to self-determination, privacy, and dignity
7. informed consent; privacy
8. competence, voluntarism, full information; comprehension
9. parent or guardian; directly benefit
10. voluntary; informed
11. egalitarian
12. reasonably informed consent

13.   (1) an explanation of the procedures to be followed and their purposes; (2) a description of the discomforts and risks to be expected; (3) a description of the benefits to be expected; (4) a disclosure of alternative procedures that might be advantageous to the participants; (5) an offer to answer any questions concerning procedures to be used; (6) an explanation that the participant may withdraw from the study at any time and suffer no negative consequences as a result

14.   (1) sensitivity of information; (2) settings being observed; (3) dissemination of information

15.   the home

16.   less widely disseminated

17.   anonymity; confidentiality

18.   Anonymity assures that nobody should be able to connect information with a specific individual. Confidentiality only means that every effort will be made to ensure that nobody connects information with a specific individual, though it is possible and in some instances inevitable. (During a personal interview, for example, the interviewer cannot help but know the respondent's answers. However, he or she should tell no one else.)

19.   F

20.   microaggregation

21.   values

22.   (1) Research data should be confidential; all participants should remain anonymous unless they (or their legal guardians) have given permission for the release of their identity. (2) Research procedures should be described fully and accurately in reports; conclusions should be objective and unbiased. (3) Informed consent should be used in obtaining participants for all research. (4) The participants should not be harmed. (5) Appropriate credit should be given to all parties contributing to the research.

Multiple-Choice Questions

1.	c		9.	d
2.	d		10.	b
3.	b		11.	c
4.	a		12.	c
5.	a		13.	a
6.	c		14.	b
7.	b		15.	c
8.	c			

True-False Questions

1.	F		6.	F
2.	T		7.	T
3.	F		8.	F
4.	T		9.	T
5.	F		10.	F

CHAPTER 5

Self-Evaluation Exercises

1. collecting, analyzing; interpreting
2. by randomly assigning subjects to experimental and control groups
3. experimental; control
4. electronic chat
5. Both variables may be caused by some third variable.
6. spurious; before
7. (1) examining both groups in terms of the dependent variable; demonstrates whether any discernible effect occurred; (2) applying an independent variable to the experimental group and withholding it from the control group; assures that the independent variable actually varies and that it occurred first; (3) making certain that background variables and test conditions are the same for both groups; assures that the relationship between variables is not spurious
8. correlated
9. experimental
10. selection
11. history
12. biological; psychological
13. experimental mortality
14. changes
15. testing
16. regression artifacts
17. interactions with selection
18. matching; randomization
19. precision matching
20. appropriate matches cannot be found

21.   frequency distribution
22.   randomization
23.   equal
24.   extrinsic; intrinsic
25.   external validity
26.   experiment, quasi-experiment; preexperiment
27.   manipulation; randomization
28.   Solomon four-group; posttest-only control-group
29.   They involve no pretesting, whereas groups in the classic experiment are pretested.
30.   sensitization
31.   It involves no pretesting.
32.   intrinsic
33.   factorial
34.   interact
35.   The effect of one variable depends on the value of another variable.
36.   simultaneous

Multiple-Choice Questions

1.	c
2.	d
3.	b
4.	a
5.	a
6.	c
7.	a
8.	d
9.	d
10.	a
11.	b
12.	b
13.	c
14.	c
15.	b

True-False Questions

1.	T
2.	F
3.	F
4.	T
5.	F
6.	T
7.	F
8.	T
9.	F
10.	T
11.	T
12.	T
13.	F
14.	T
15.	F

CHAPTER 6

Self-Evaluation Exercises

1.   social, political; ethical
2.   stimulus; response; property; disposition
3.   (1) The interval between stimulus and response is usually quite short compared to that between a property and a disposition. (2) Stimuli are usually more specific than properties. (3) Stimulus-response groups are often equivalent, whereas property-disposition groups often differ on several crucial variables. (4) It is usually easier to tell whether a stimulus precedes a response than it is to tell whether a property precedes a disposition.
4.   correlational
5.   They make use of multivariate methods of statistical analysis.
6.   properties; dispositions
7.   multivariate methods; path analysis
8.   (1) They are carried out in natural settings. (2) They permit the use of random probability samples.
9.   randomization
10.   preexperiments; experiments
11.   groups
12.   (1) obtain supplementary evidence; (2) use a nonequivalent control group design; (3) match units from the contrasted groups on one or more background variables; (4) take several measures of the dependent variable
13.   nonequivalent control group design
14.   equally
15.   time-series design
16.   (1) obtaining an initial sample of respondents who will agree to be interviewed over an extended time period; (2) subsequent dropout (mortality of subjects who initially agreed to participate in the study); (3) panel conditioning, whereby subjects become sensitized to repeated measurements
17.   three; independent
18.   by obtaining multiple measurements of a dependent variable before and after introduction of the independent variable
19.   If an independent variable is introduced after an unstable trend line has reached an extreme point, it is difficult to know whether subsequent changes resulted from the independent variable or the tendency of the trend to regress toward a less extreme point.
20.   some comparison groups roughly similar to the groups of interest
21.   experimental; quasi-experimental

22. (1) They are not suitable for experimental manipulation. (2) They do not allow for random assignment to experimental and control groups. (3) They provide no basis for comparison. (4) They are unable to control for sources of invalidity, external or internal.
23. exploratory
24. a pretest
25. case survey method
26. Nonexperimental designs, of which surveys are a typical example, lack the internal validity that characterizes experiments, which use randomization to rule out threats to internal validity. By contrast, surveys generally rely on representative samples and avoid the "artificiality" of laboratory settings. Thus surveys are more externally valid than experiments.

Multiple-Choice Questions   *True-False Questions*

1.   a   1.   F
2.   c   2.   F
3.   d   3.   F
4.   c   4.   T
5.   b   5.   T
6.   c   6.   F
7.   d   7.   T
8.   d   8.   T
9.   d   9.   F
10. c   10. T
11. d
12. a
13. c
14. b
15. a

CHAPTER 7

Self-Evaluation Exercises

1.   (1) numerals; (2) numbers; (3) other symbols
2.   numbers
3.   mapping
4.   how numbers are assigned to objects or events
5.   isomorphic

6.   direct; indicators
7.   inferential
8.   nominal, ordinal, interval; ratio
9.   nominal
10.   exhaustive; mutually exclusive
11.   ordinal
12.   separated by equal intervals
13.   zero
14.   real differences
15.   (1) Scores may be related to an associated attribute. (2) Differences may be due to differences in temporary conditions. (3) People may interpret the measurement instrument differently. (4) The setting in which the measure is used may differ. (5) The administration of the measurement may differ.
16.   systematic; random
17.   one is measuring what one thinks one is measuring
18.   content validity, empirical validity; construct validity
19.   Face
20.   all aspects of the phenomenon being measured are included in the measurement
21.   empirical
22   construct validity
23.   true component; error component; reliability
24.   completely in error
25.   test-retest; parallel-forms; split-half
26.   (1) The first measurement may have affected the thing being measured. (2) Many phenomena change rapidly, so that assessments made at two different times show a difference, but one that is not due to unreliability.
27.   parallel-forms
28.   split-half

Multiple-Choice Questions		*True-False Questions*	
1.	d	1.	F
2.	b	2.	T
3.	a	3.	F
4.	c	4.	F
5.	d	5.	T
6.	a	6.	F
7.	c	7.	T
8.	d	8.	T
9.	b	9.	F
10.	a	10.	T
11.	b	11.	T
12.	c	12.	T
13.	a	13.	F
14.	b	14.	T
15.	d	15.	F

CHAPTER 8

Self-Evaluation Exercises

1.   generalizations; population
2.   it is impractical or impossible to study all cases of a population
3.   parameter; statistic
4.   population
5.   sampling unit
6.   finite
7.   sampling frames
8.   incomplete
9.   clusters
10.   blank foreign elements
11.   The sampling frames (telephone directories, club membership lists, and magazine subscription lists) underrepresented poor people, who voted overwhelmingly for Roosevelt.
12.   as representative of the population from which it is drawn as possible
13.   Because sampling elements are randomly selected, probability samples are able to specify the chance each case has of being chosen for the sample. In nonprobability sampling, there is no way to estimate the likelihood of cases being included in the sample.

14. Two reasons are convenience and economy, which in certain situations could outweigh the advantages of probability sampling. Also, circumstances may make the use of probability sampling impossible, such as when a list of the sampling population is unavailable.
15. convenience
16. purposive
17. (1) It is impossible to estimate sampling errors. (2) Interviewers may pick unrepresentative samples within quota groups. (3) They make control of fieldwork difficult.
18. simple random sampling, systematic sampling, stratified sampling; cluster sampling
19. 50/300 or .17
20. more convenient and easier to execute
21. If the sampling frame has a particular pattern, or if the population is listed or arranged in a systematic way, the sample could be unrepresentative.
22. stratified
23. disproportionate
24. (1) It is less expensive than many other sample designs. (2) It is an effective method of sampling from a large and geographically dispersed population.
25. what level of accuracy is desired and how much error is acceptable
26. standard error (or sampling error)
27. standard deviation of the sample; square root of the sample size
28. the sample is a substantial fraction of the population
29. confidence interval
30. (1) 68 percent; (2) about 95 percent
31. large
32. nonresponse
33. The nonrespondents (those who could not have been included in the sample because they were excluded from the sampling frames) mostly voted for Roosevelt, whereas respondents gave most of their votes to Landon.
34. uninterviewables, not found, not-at-homes; refusals

Multiple-Choice Questions

1.	c	9.	b
2.	d	10.	d
3.	c	11.	a
4.	d	12.	a
5.	c	13.	d
6.	a	14.	d
7.	d	15.	b
8.	b		

True-False Questions

1.	T		9.	T
2.	F		10.	F
3.	F		11.	F
4.	F		12.	T
5.	F		13.	T
6.	T		14.	F
7.	F		15.	F
8.	F			

CHAPTER 9

Self-Evaluation Exercises

1. observation
2. survey research, secondary data analysis; qualitative research
3. formal; informal; verbal; nonverbal
4. the use of two or more methods of data collection
5. directness
6. natural settings
7. (1) what to observe; (2) when to observe and (3) how to record observations; how much inference is required
8. nonverbal behavior
9. how individuals structure the space around them
10. extralinguistic behavior
11. representative of ongoing occurrences
12. infrequently
13. deductive
14. empirical
15. explicit, exhaustive; mutually exclusive
16. Examples include specific kinds of speech, such as asking questions, that may underlie a motive.
17. Many body movements, such as head-shaking (which could indicate disapproval, doubt, or difficulty in comprehension), require a *high* level of inference.
18. controlled; noncontrolled
19. laboratory; field
20. (1) They allow for thorough control of extrinsic and intrinsic factors. (2) They provide unambiguous information about causation.

21.   experimental realism
22.   experimental subjects, knowing they are being observed, respond more to their interpretation of what responses are desired from them than to the experimental stimulus
23.   deception
24.   experimenter bias
25.   by preventing experimenter interaction with participants through the use of tape recorders, videotape presentations, and the like, or by using experimenters with different expectations
26.   experimenter bias; measurement artifacts
27.   extrinsic
28.   field experiments take place in more "real-world" natural settings
29.   the lack of control the researcher has over intrinsic and (especially) extrinsic factors

Multiple-Choice Questions   *True-False Questions*

1.	c		1.	F
2.	d		2.	T
3.	c		3.	T
4.	c		4.	F
5.	b		5.	T
6.	b		6.	F
7.	b		7.	F
8.	b		8.	F
9.	c		9.	T
10.	a		10.	T
11.	d			
12.	a			
13.	d			
14.	a			
15.	c			

CHAPTER 10

Self-Evaluation Exercises

1.   observe directly
2.   personal interviews, mail questionnaires; telephone surveys
3.   their low cost
4.   biasing

5. low response rate

6. Mail questionnaire response rates tend to be low, and nonrespondents tend to differ from respondents. Thus our ability to generalize is hindered.

7. (1) Get sponsorship by an organization known to respondents. (2) Include a token remuneration with the questionnaire. (3) In general, keep it short. (4) Write an attractive cover letter containing an appeal to altruism. (5) Send along a self-addressed, stamped envelope. (6) Choose a well-educated group of interested professionals. (7) Send out two waves of follow-ups, or more.

8. typography, format, spacing and margins, paper quality

9. Often nonrespondents are less well-educated than respondents. Also, nonrespondents tend to be very mobile and therefore more difficult to locate than respondents.

10. the Total Design Method

11. (1) In sending follow-up mailings only to those respondents who did not reply to the first mailing, one must be able to identify all respondents; therefore, anonymity cannot be guaranteed. (2) Those who reply after follow-up mailings may take the study less seriously than the initial respondents and may fill out the questionnaire hurriedly or return an incomplete questionnaire. Because of these possibilities, the data obtained from follow-ups may be somewhat unreliable.

12. schedule-structured

13. respondents; interviewers or other conditions of the interview

14. Unlike schedule-structured interviews, in which the wording and sequence of questions is fixed for all respondents, nonscheduled interviews do not employ a specified set of questions. Also, using nonscheduled interviews, the interviewer has greater liberty in probing respondents for additional information.

15. (1) control of the interview situation; (2) high response rate; (3) collection of supplementary information; (4) greater flexibility

16. (1) higher cost; (2) the possibility of interviewer bias; (3) lack of anonymity

17. (1) making respondents believe that the interview will be pleasant and satisfying; (2) making respondents see that this study is worthwhile; (3) overcoming barriers to the interview in the mind of the respondent

18. (1) The questionnaire should be followed, although it can be used informally. (2) The interview should be informal and relaxed. (3) Questions should be asked as worded in the questionnaire. (4) Questions should be asked in the sequence as they appear on the questionnaire. (5) Questions that appear to be misunderstood by the respondent should be repeated.

19. probing

20. (1) to motivate the respondent to elaborate or clarify his or her response; (2) to focus the conversation on the specific topic of the interview

21. less structured interviews

22. semipersonal
23. serious sampling bias
24. random-digit dialing
25. (1) Respondents are more likely to terminate the interview before it is complete. (2) Interviewers cannot describe the respondent's environment. (3) Respondents feel uncomfortable discussing some topics on the telephone.
26. (1) mail; (2) telephone; (3) personal interview; (4) telephone; (5) mail; (6) personal interview

Multiple-Choice Questions

1.	c			
2.	b			
3.	c			
4.	d			
5.	c			
6.	d			
7.	a			
8.	a			
9.	a			
10.	c			
11.	c			
12.	c			
13.	a			
14.	b			
15.	c			
16.	a			
17.	a			
18.	b			
19.	d			
20.	d			

True-False Questions

1.	F
2.	T
3.	T
4.	F
5.	F
6.	T
7.	F
8.	T
9.	T
10.	T

CHAPTER 11

Self-Evaluation Exercises

1. questions; motivating
2. factual; opinion and attitude
3. objective
4. (1) They do not know the information. (2) They cannot recall the information. (3) They do not understand the question. (4) They are reluctant to answer.
5. attitudes
6. content, directions; intensity
7. attitudes have more than one dimension
8. wording, emphasis; sequence
9. open-ended, closed-ended; contingency
10. (1) They are easy to ask and answer. (2) Analysis is straightforward.
11. They may introduce bias by forcing respondents to select from a pre-fixed set of answers, none of which the respondent may feel is exactly appropriate or correct.
12. (1) They allow respondents to answer in their own words. (2) They are flexible and provide more opportunities for probing.
13. They may be difficult for respondents to understand, and the researcher may have difficulty analyzing and interpreting responses.
14. (1) to learn about processes by which one comes to a particular point of view; (2) to see whether the respondent really knows anything about the object of the question; (3) to study attitudes that are not fully crystallized; (4) to elicit answers from those not highly motivated to respond
15. when certain questions apply to some respondents but not to others
16. filter
17. Circle a number. It is self-coding, and it is clear which answer the respondent selected. Checking a blank is least preferred. It may result in respondents marking between the blanks, making it difficult to tell which response was intended.
18. rating scale
19. intensity
20. ordinal
21. presenting a number of questions that have the same response categories
22. rank
23. funnel
24. obtain detailed information

25. the topic doesn't motivate the respondent to communicate, or the purpose is to obtain generalizations
26. questions that are easy to answer, interesting, and nonthreatening
27. open-ended questions, questions that require more time and thought, and questions dealing with sensitive issues
28. eight
29. response set
30. all questions in a set have the same response format, especially if they all refer to the same topic
31. changing the question format by varying the response categories for each question or avoiding lumping together questions referring to the same topic
32. leading
33. response bias, whether by denial of the behavior in question or by underreporting
34. They can be confusing to a respondent who may agree with one part of the question but disagree with another. They may also make it difficult for the researcher to interpret responses, since he or she doesn't know which part of the question respondents were answering.
35. In personal interviews, the interviewer is present and may be able to overcome resistance to the questionnaire. The cover letter is the only device for encouraging the respondent to respond to a questionnaire.
36. (1) identification of the organization sponsoring the study; (2) explanation of the purpose of the study; (3) a statement of why it is important for the respondent to complete and return the questionnaire; (4) assurance of confidentiality
37. self-explanatory

Multiple-Choice Questions

1.	c		9.	c
2.	c		10.	a
3.	a		11.	d
4.	b		12.	a
5.	a		13.	b
6.	c		14.	b
7.	b			
8.	c			

True-False Questions

1.	F		6.	F
2.	T		7.	T
3.	T		8.	F
4.	F		9.	F
5.	T		10.	F

CHAPTER 12

Self-Evaluation Exercises

1. field research; *Verstehen*
2. the study of people acting in the natural courses of their daily lives
3. its location (in natural settings) and by the manner in which it is conducted
4. participant observation
5. When the researcher acts as complete participant, his or her role as observer is concealed from the persons under study. As participant-as-observer, the researcher's role is known to the group being studied and the research goal is explicitly defined.
6. (1) The observer may be so concerned about making correct observations that he or she is unable to act convincingly as a complete participant. (2) The researcher must be careful in asking questions or otherwise evoking responses in such a way that would reveal his or her identity as an observer. (3) Field notes of behavior cannot be recorded on the spot. On the other hand, postponement in recording field notes may result in distortions.
7. (1) selecting a topic; (2) choosing a research site and gaining access; (3) establishing relations with members; (4) leaving the field; (5) recording observations; (6) analyzing data
8. Depending on the nature of the research topic and the group being studied, researchers may be more successful in gaining access to and establishing rapport with members of a group if they share the personal attributes of the members. On the other hand, some studies have shown that researchers with different attributes (e.g., gender, race) than those of the group as threatening.
9. negative cases

10.   Analytic induction is a theoretical approach to field research in which the researcher attempts to verify a tentative hypothesis by observing a small number of cases. If the hypothesis does not explain or account for the cases observed, the hypothesis is modified until the observations are successfully explained.

11.   (1) Deception. Some claim that conducting fieldwork under a false or concealed identity is dishonest and amounts to an unjustified invasion of privacy. Others contend that deception is sometimes necessary to gain access to certain groups and that concealment of the researcher's identity does not cause harm to those who are studied. (2) Impact on those studied. Aside from the issue of deception, some social scientists claim that field research can have potentially harmful, if unintended, effects on those being studied. Such effects may occur if, for example, an observer is falsely perceived as having powers to bestow benefits on or improve living conditions for the person being studied. Later awareness that the researcher does not possess such powers could have an adverse psychological impact on those under observation.

Multiple-Choice Questions		*True-False Questions*	
1.	c	1.	F
2.	d	2.	F
3.	d	3.	F
4.	a	4.	T
5.	a	5.	F
6.	c	6.	T
7.	b	7.	F
8.	b	8.	F
9.	d	9.	T
10.	d	10.	T
11.	a		
12.	c		
13.	a		
14.	b		
15.	d		

CHAPTER 13

Self-Evaluation Exercises

1.   secondary data
2.   (1) conceptual-substantive; (2) methodological; (3) economic
3.   (1) Often secondary data only approximate the kind of data the researcher would ideally like to have. (2) Sometimes the researcher has limited access to secondary data, either because it is difficult to locate the data to meet the researcher's exact needs or because other investigators are unwilling to release data they possess. (3) Sometimes the researcher lacks sufficient information about a body of secondary data to tell if the data are accurate and unbiased.
4.   the recording of demographic data of a population in a defined territory made by the government at a specific time and at regular intervals
5.   A complete count census provides data for an entire defined population. Thus, it eliminates problems that are a result of sampling error. On the other hand, a complete count census is very expensive, administratively complex, and can be used to collect only the most basic of data. A sample census, while surveying only a segment of a population, is cheaper and more efficient and is able to obtain a larger body of data.
6.   Metropolitan Statistical Area (MSA)
7.   Census tracts
8.   10
9.   (1) specification of needs; (2) familiarization; (3) initial contacts; (4) secondary contacts; (5) accessibility; (6) analysis and supplemental analyses
10. on-line
11. regulate
12. any method of data collection that removes the researcher from the interactions, events, or behavior being investigated
13. erosion
14. accretion
15. (1) exterior body and physical signs; (2) expressive movement; (3) physical location analysis; (4) language behavior
16. expressive movement
17. actuarial records
18. (1) *A Review of Elections of the World*; (2) *America at the Polls*
19. (1) autobiography; (2) diary; (3) letters
20. deliberate deception; unconscious misrepresentation
21. data analysis; observation

22. The researcher "asks questions" not of people but of people's communications. Thus, there is no contact or direct interaction with the persons whose communications are to be studied.
23. (1) newspaper articles; (2) song lyrics; (3) personal correspondence; (4) speeches; (5) private notes; (6) public documents; (7) books; (8) any other recording of the printed or spoken word
24. (1) words or terms; (2) themes; (3) characters; (4) paragraphs; (5) items

Multiple-Choice Questions

1. c
2. a
3. c
4. b
5. d
6. c
7. a
8. b
9. d
10. d
11. b
12. a
13. c
14. a
15. b

True-False Questions

1. T
2. F
3. T
4. F
5. T
6. F
7. F
8. F
9. F
10. T

CHAPTER 14

Self-Evaluation Exercises

1. code
2. classify responses into meaningful categories
3. data are recorded according to a preconceived theory
4. the coding scheme is designed on the basis of a representative sample or on other data that are not based on theory
5. exhaustive
6. mutually exclusive
7. A codebook is a document that records each variable's name and number, where each is located, the coding scheme, and codes for missing data.

8. coded; analysis
9. open-ended; closed-ended
10. (1) Different coders may arrive at different interpretations of responses. (2) Coders and respondents may interpret responses differently.
11. less
12. (1) transfer sheets—data are transferred to computer forms that resemble old computer cards; (2) edge codes—data are transferred directly onto spaces at the outside edge of the instrument; (3) optical scanning—data are read into the computer by a special instrument; (4) direct data entry—data are entered directly into the computer
13. coding; keying; reliability
14. direct data entry; computer-assisted telephone interviewing (CATI)
15. data cleaning; special computer programs
16. (1) mainframe computers; (2) personal computers
17. mainframe; time-sharing
18. software
19. personal computer (PC)

Multiple-Choice Questions

1. b
2. c
3. d
4. b
5. a
6. b
7. d
8. c
9. a
10. c

True-False Questions

1. T
2. F
3. T
4. T
5. F
6. T
7. F
8. T
9. T
10. F

CHAPTER 15

Self-Evaluation Exercises

1. Descriptive
2. inferential

3.   frequency distribution
4.   Republican 56
      Democrat   102
      Independent 36
      None 6
5.   proportions; percentages
6.   Cityview has the greatest number of armed robberies; however, armed robbery as a percentage of total crime is highest in Podunk.
7.   Graphs
8.   pie chart; bar chart
9.   histogram
10.   histogram
11.   measure of central tendency
12.   mode, median; arithmetic mean
13.   mode
14.   can be easily identified
15.   median
16.   75th percentile
17.   arithmetic mean
18.   summing; number of cases
19.   sensitive to extreme scores
20.   (1) mean; (2) mode; (3) median; (4) mean; (5) mode
21.   variation or scatter; central value
22.   measure of qualitative variation
23.   maximum distribution in a nominal distribution
24.   highest; lowest
25.   it takes into account only the two extreme values in the distribution
26.   it measures the degree of spread in the middle half of a distribution
27.   zero
28.   standard deviation
29.   original units
30.   coefficient of variation
31.   symmetrical
32.   skewed
33.   symmetrical
34.   negatively
35.   infinite
36.   13.6%
37.   mean; standard deviation
38.   zero

Multiple-Choice Questions

1. b
2. b
3. b
4. a
5. c
6. d
7. d
8. a
9. c
10. a
11. a
12. c
13. c
14. d
15. c

True-False Questions

1. T
2. T
3. F
4. T
5. T
6. T
7. F
8. F
9. F
10. T

CHAPTER 16

Self-Evaluation Exercises

1. examining patterns of relationships between variables
2. categories or values of one variable go with certain categories or values of another variable
3. bivariate table
4. independent; dependent
5. univariate
6. unrelated or independent
7. mode
8. (1) 61.5%; (2) 37.5%; (3) 250; (4) 1,700; (5) yes
9. one variable predicts another
10. before introducing an independent variable; after introducing an independent variable
11. asymmetrical; zero; one
12. nominal variables
13. the independent variable eliminates 50 percent of the errors in predicting the dependent variable
14. mode

15.   positive
16.   negative (or inverse)
17.   the two variables are unrelated
18.   pair
19.   asymmetrical; a perfect negative (inverse) relationship; a perfect positive relationship
20.   its exclusion of tied pairs from computation
21.   tau-*b*
22.   precise predictions
23.   a straight line
24.   the intercept (or the value of Y when X is zero); the steepness of the slope (the direction and strength of the relationship between X and Y)
25.   57.8%
26.   mean
27.   scatter diagram
28.   the amount of prediction error resulting from use of a regression equation or the unexplained variation around a regression line
29.   zero
30.   amount of variation in a dependent variable explained by an independent variable
31.   the degree of spread of actual observations around a regression line

Multiple-Choice Questions   *True-False Questions*

1.	c		1.	T
2.	b		2.	F
3.	b		3.	F
4.	a		4.	F
5.	d		5.	T
6.	a		6.	F
7.	c		7.	F
8.	b		8.	T
9.	d		9.	T
10.	b		10.	F
11.	a			
12.	c			
13.	d			
14.	a			
15.	b			

CHAPTER 17

Self-Evaluation Exercises

1.   (1) control—determining whether a bivariate relationship is spurious; (2) elaboration—clarifying a bivariate relationship by examining intervening or conditional variables; (3) prediction—analyzing two or more independent variables to see how much variation in the dependent variable they account for.

2.   spurious

3.   In social research, control is the process of ascertaining whether covariation between an independent variable and a dependent variable is genuine or whether such variation is spurious, i.e., accounted for by extraneous factors. In quasi-experimental research designs, control is a statistical operation whereby one examines not only the original bivariate relationship, but also the relationship between the independent and dependent variables and some third or extraneous variable.

4.   cross-tabulation, partial correlation; multiple regression

5.   In experiments, control is accomplished through random assignment of subjects to experimental and control groups so that both groups are as much alike as possible and that they will differ only with respect to their exposure to the independent variable. In quasi-experiments, in which it is not possible to assign subjects to experimental and control groups, control takes the form of statistical manipulations.

6.   cross-tabulations; matching

7.   partial

8.   (1) examining an original bivariate relationship (constructing a bivariate table); (2) identifying a possible control variable; (3) dividing the sample into subgroups according to categories of the control variable; (4) constructing partial tables and reanalyzing the bivariate relationship within categories of the control variable

9.   When analyzed within categories of the control variable, the original bivariate relationship would have to disappear.

10.   It requires relatively large samples. Otherwise, each additional control variable further reduces the number of cases on which analyses are based.

11.   Control is a process of determining whether a bivariate relationship is spurious. Elaboration is a process of introducing additional variables to clarify the precise nature of an observed relationship.

12.   An intervening variable is one which, at least logically, occurs "between" the independent and dependent variables. A conditional variable is one which clarifies an original relationship by giving insight as to the circumstances (conditions) under which the relationship occurs.

13.   a specification of conditions or contingencies necessary for the occurrence of the

        relationship

14.   control variable

15.   (1) variables that specify associations in terms of interest and concern; (2) variables that specify associations in terms of time and place; (3) background characteristics of the units of analysis

16.   the amount of correlation between two variables while controlling for a third variable

17.   first-order partial

18. r_{123}

19. Y: predicted values of the dependent variable
        a: the intercept point on the Y axis for X_1 and X_2
        $b_1 x_1$: the amount of change in Y associated with x_1 while controlling for x_2
        $b_2 x_2$: the amount of change in Y associated with x_2 while controlling for x_1

20.   linear

21.   beta weights

22.   the amount of change in the dependent variable with one unit of change in the dependent variable while controlling for all other variables in the regression equation

23.   the combined effect of two or more independent variables on a dependent variable

24.   (1) the time sequence of the independent and dependent variables; (2) the size of the partial correlations

25.   (1) There can be no two-way causation. (2) No variable can cause other variables preceding it in the causal sequence.

26.   (1) There is no two-way causation between X and Y. (2) x_4 is alleged to be a cause of a preceding variable, x_2.

27.   path analysis

28.   Residual variables are those variables which express variation in a dependent variable unaccounted for by specified independent variables in a causal model.

Multiple-Choice Questions		*True-False Questions*	
1.	b	1.	F
2.	a	2.	T
3.	c	3.	F
4.	b	4.	T
5.	d	5.	T
6.	b	6.	F
7.	c	7.	T
8.	a	8.	F
9.	b	9.	F
10.	c	10.	F
11.	c	11.	F
12.	c	12.	T
13.	a	13.	F
14.	d	14.	T
15.	d	15.	F

CHAPTER 18

Self-Evaluation Exercises

1.   measurement
2.   indicators
3.   (1) to reduce the complexity of data; (2) to produce precise measures amenable to statistical manipulation; (3) to increase the reliability of measures
4.   Indexes are simpler and easier to construct. Scales are more rigorous, more complex, and require greater attention to issues of reliability and validity.
5.   (1) defining the purpose for constructing an index; (2) selecting sources of data for an index; (3) selecting a base; (4) selecting methods of aggregation and weighting
6.   A simple aggregate is merely a sum of the individual components of an index. A weighted aggregate takes into account the relative influence (weight) of the various components.
7.   There is no procedure for ensuring that the various items in the scale all tap the same dimension.
8.   attitudes
9.   (1) compiling possible scale items; (2) administering items to a random sample of respondents; (3) computing a total score for each respondent; (4) determining the discriminative power of scale items; (5) selecting scale items; (6) testing reliability

10. unidimensional; cumulative
11. coefficient of reproducibility
12. .85
13. classify a large number of interrelated variables into a smaller number of dimensions or factors
14. factor loading

Multiple-Choice Questions		*True-False Questions*	
1.	c	1.	T
2.	b	2.	F
3.	b	3.	T
4.	c	4.	F
5.	a	5.	T
6.	c	6.	F
7.	d	7.	F
8.	d	8.	T
9.	a	9.	T
10.	d	10.	F

CHAPTER 19

Self-Evaluation Exercises

1. hypothesis testing
2. formulate it in statistical terms
3. H_0
4. antithesis
5. This fallacy concludes that, if A predicts B and B subsequently occurs, then A was true, despite the fact that there may be any number of other reasons why B occurred.
6. sampling distribution
7. region of rejection
8. level of significance
9. 5
10. one-tailed
11. two-tailed
12. Type I; Type II

13. probability of making a Type I error (rejecting a true null hypothesis)
14. decreases
15. .05, .01; .001
16. parametric test
17. (1) Observations must come from a normally distributed population. (2) The variables are measured on an interval or ratio scale.
18. nonparametric
19. $H_0:2 = 3$
20. each sample size is greater than 30
21. n is less than or equal to 30
22. 2.456; 2.145; 2.845; 2.819; 1.684
23. $t = 4.81$; $H_1:m\ F$; $H_0: m\ F$
24. Yes; $Z = 3.30$, which is much larger than the critical value of $Z = 1.96$ (for a two-tailed test); if a one-tailed test is conducted, critical $Z = 1.65$.
25. $Z = 1.7325$, which is small enough so that the null hypothesis must be accepted
26. $Z = 1.7325$, which allows us to reject the null hypothesis at the .05 level of significance (the critical value of Z is 1.65)
27. $U = 9$, and the critical value for U is 12. We may therefore conclude that the null hypothesis should be rejected, and that Republicans are more likely than Democrats to be rated favorably.
28. two nominal variables are cross-classified
29. 12
30. chi-square $= 59.32$, with 4 degrees of freedom. The critical value is 13.277. Consequently, we would reject the null hypothesis that political and voting intentions are unrelated and accept the conclusion that they are related.

Multiple-Choice Questions

1. c
2. c
3. a
4. b
5. d
6. d
7. d
8. a
9. d
10. a
11. c
12. b

True-False Questions

1. T
2. T
3. T
4. F
5. T
6. T
7. F
8. F
9. F
10. F
11. F
12. F

Multiple-Choice Questions	True-False Questions
13. b	13. T
14. c	14. T
15. a	